THE SEVEN LAWS OF CHRISTIAN LEADERSHIP

I. EXAMPLE:
PEOPLE NEED TO BE ABLE TO DEPEND
ON YOUR LEADERSHIP

II. COMMUNICATION:
PEOPLE NEED TO KNOW WHAT YOU ARE SAYING

III. ABILITY:
YOU NEED TO BE CAPABLE OF LEADING OTHER PEOPLE

IV. MOTIVATION:
YOU NEED TO KNOW WHY YOU WANT TO BE A LEADER

V. AUTHORITY:
PEOPLE NEED TO RESPOND TO YOUR LEADERSHIP

VI. STRATEGY:
YOU NEED TO KNOW WHERE YOU ARE GOING

VII. LOVE:
YOU NEED TO CARE FOR THE PEOPLE AROUND YOU

THE SEVEN LAWS OF CHRISTIAN LEADERSHIP

DAVID HOCKING

THE SEVEN LAWS OF CHRISTIAN LEADERSHIP

HOW TO INSPIRE PEOPLE TO FOLLOW WHEN YOU ARE CALLED TO LEAD

Regal Books

A Division of GL Publications
Ventura, California, U.S.A.

Published by Regal Books
A Division of GL Publications
Ventura, California 93006
Printed in U.S.A.

Library of Congress Cataloging-in-Publication Data
Hocking, David L.
    [Be a leader people follow]
    The 7 laws of Christian leadership / David Hocking.
    p. cm.
    Previously published under title: Be a leader people follow.
    ©1979.
    ISBN 0-8307-1461-8
    1. Christian leadership. I. Hocking, David L. Be a leader people
      follow. II. Title. III. Title: Seven laws of Christian leadership.
    BV652.1.H58 1991
    253—dc20   91-13138
                                             CIP

1 2 3 4 5 6 7 8 9 10 / KP / X3.0 / 95 94 93 92 91

Rights for publishing this book in other languages are contracted by
Gospel Literature International (GLINT) foundation. GLINT also pro-
vides technical help for the adaptation, translation, and publishing
of Bible study resources and books in scores of languages worldwide.
For further information, contact GLINT, Post Office Box 488,
Rosemead, California, 91770, U.S.A., or the publisher.

TO the members of churches where I have served as pastor who have watched me grow in my desire to serve the Lord, patiently enduring my struggles with spiritual leadership, I dedicate this book.

To those scores of faithful staff members with whom I have served these many years and who know my weaknesses as a spiritual leader, yet have supported and loved me in spite of it all, I dedicate this book.

To the students who sat under my teaching of leadership and often wondered if I knew what I was talking about, I dedicate this book.

To spiritual leaders everywhere who, like me, desire to be more effective in their leadership of God's people and understand their need of help, I dedicate this book.

CONTENTS

LAW IV—MOTIVATION:
You Need to Know Why You Want to Be a Leader

LAW V—AUTHORITY:
People Need to Respond to Your Leadership

LAW VI—STRATEGY:
You Need to Know Where You Are Going

LAW VII—LOVE:
You Need to Care for the People Around You

PREFACE

IT was in the third grade in a military academy where I learned to swim. The instructor made me jump in the pool at the deep end. It is amazing how quickly one can learn to adjust to the problems of life! I have never forgotten that lesson. The instructor knew more about me than I thought at that time. He knew that with me it was "sink or swim." Leadership is like that—some of us have to learn the hard way!

Like most people, I have been exposed to various leadership responsibilities (some of which I would like to forget!). Through them all, I have often wondered what makes a good leader. From the joys and heartaches of starting a church and watching it grow to my present responsibilities as senior pastor of a large church and school system with many employees and a large operating budget, I still wonder what it takes to make a good leader! Even though I have taught leadership to graduate school students, I still wonder.

Without God's help, none of us could ever hope to be what God describes as a spiritual leader. It seems that two out of every three decisions I make don't turn out the way I thought. However, I have learned some valuable principles and have put them down on paper. Maybe you need to do the same. Some things are essentials in this matter of leadership, and other things you can take or leave. It is my prayer that you will study the essentials I have listed in this book in the light of what God's Word teaches and your own experience verifies. Perhaps you will agree that these things are necessary and will make us all better leaders.

In this revision, I have added several chapters that I believe will not only broaden the scope of our understanding of spiritual leadership, but will also strengthen our resolve to be what God wants us to be.

David Hocking
1991

LAW I

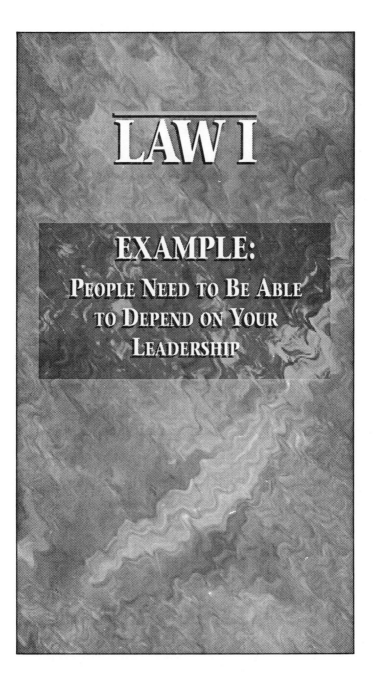

EXAMPLE:

PEOPLE NEED TO BE ABLE TO DEPEND ON YOUR LEADERSHIP

1

WHAT KIND OF AN EXAMPLE SHOULD A SPIRITUAL LEADER BE?

M Y first idea of a leader was my dad. He was strong and believed in discipline. He loved people and often helped them in time of need. He was not well-educated, but he seemed to understand people. He was committed to the Lord's work and gave freely of his money to support it. I remember his hands. They were rough from the hours of hard labor he experienced in the oil fields. His hands were always doing things, and sometimes it seemed to me as a boy that my dad's character was in those hands. They still remind me of who he was and what he did. He now is with the Lord.

Next came my pastor. He was soft-spoken, loving and kind. He always seemed to have time for people. When he preached, he seemed to be talking with you as though you were the only one in the auditorium. He constantly encouraged me and followed my growth in the Lord. When I was away in college, he wrote me letters. I had the joy of working with him on his staff and observing him up close. What an honor!

Many others along the way manifested leadership to me, but the day came when I needed answers to some questions: What is a spiritual leader? How do you know one when you see one? What was God's idea of a leader? So I had to turn to the Bible for answers and I started with the Old Testament.

OLD TESTAMENT EXAMPLES OF LEADERSHIP

Moses

The first Old Testament figure to capture my attention was Moses. In Exodus 18 he received some good advice from his father-in-law, Jethro, who was a priest of Midian. Jethro told him that he was wearing himself out by trying to handle everything himself. The people were also weary of this method. Whenever you see a situation like this, where one person is trying to do it all himself, there is a need for leadership.

One of the fallacies of human nature is that we do not see ourselves as others see us. We do not like to admit there is something we cannot do. If the situation, like that of Moses, does not change and responsibilities are not shared with others, then the "Peter Principle" sets in very quickly. That principle of modern business deals with people rising to their level of incompetence! The tragedy is that many people cannot face this fact. As a result, they become the major obstacle to further growth or progress.

I can identify easily with Moses. I would rather do it

myself than have others do it. But that doesn't mean that I do it better! In fact, I have often suffered because I did not allow others to help. When it comes down to the bottom line, it's usually an ego problem. I don't want to admit that I can't handle a situation, or I want others to see how capable I really am!

The first thing Moses had to do was to clarify his own job description. Job descriptions should always begin at

---

Too often the main leader becomes wrapped up in details that other workers should handle.

---

the top and work down through other levels in the organization. They should be simple, clear, and flexible. According to Exodus 18:19-21, Moses had three major responsibilities: (1) to bring the problems of the people to God; (2) to teach them the way they should walk and train them in the work they are to do; (3) to select able leaders to help him bear the burden of leadership.

Sound simple? That's the way it should be! Too often the main leader becomes wrapped up in details that other workers should handle, thus diminishing the effectiveness of his own life and responsibilities. Sometimes, as in the case of Moses, it is hard to let go of things you are doing until someone in whom you have confidence explains to you the danger of trying to do it all yourself.

At one point in my ministry I was following the "Moses syndrome." I was not delegating to others and, frankly, I was exhausted by the many things I was doing. A trusted friend and co-worker came to me one day and said, "David, what will we ever do when you die?" That did it. It was hard to admit, but I was the problem. Too much depended upon me, and I was not indispensable. We made some immediate changes that resulted in continued growth.

Moses also had to know what qualities to look for in leaders who could help him (see Exod. 18:21). He had to look for (1) men who feared God, (2) men of truth and (3) men who hated dishonest gain.

There is no reference in these qualifications to educational background or any particular skills or talents. These qualities represent men who can be trusted and followed. It is a godly life-style that counts!

Joshua

After Moses died, the Lord spoke to Joshua and told him that he would lead His people to the land which He was giving them. Deuteronomy 34:9 says that Joshua had been chosen by Moses to take his place.

Joshua was "filled with the spirit of wisdom." In Joshua 1 there is a list of qualifications he would need for effective leadership: (1) spiritual strength and courage (see Josh. 1:6,7,9); (2) constant meditation in God's Word (see Josh. 1:8); and (3) uncompromising obedience to God's commands (see Josh. 1:7,8). God said that if these qualities were in Joshua's life, he could expect prosperity and success.

Too many Christian leaders today are trying to operate in their own strength and are compromising on the plain teaching of the Word of God. Joshua was told, "Do not turn from it to the right or to the left." Any slight departure or deviation from God's Word will result in a loss of leadership at that point.

Many years ago I had a friend in the ministry who

began to deviate from God's Word in a certain area. We talked about it and even prayed together. For a time, his leadership continued to be strong and well supported. He justified violating the Word of God on the basis of what appeared to be the blessing of God upon his ministry. God was patient with him, and gave him many opportunities to get right with Him.

One thing led to another and before too long he developed a pattern of violating the Word of God. I was not surprised to learn of his departure from the ministry and the failure of his leadership in a critical situation. We must learn the lesson God revealed to Joshua. Success according to God is based upon uncompromising obedience to His Word.

David

God chose David as a leader because he had internal strength. When Samuel came to anoint one of Jesse's sons to be king of Israel, he took one look at Eliab and thought, "Surely the Lord's anointed is before Him" (1 Sam. 16:6). However, God responded: "Do not look at his appearance or at the height of his stature, because I have rejected him; for God sees not as man sees, for man looks at the outward appearance, but the Lord looks at the heart" (v. 7).

How true that is! In choosing a leader, we look for the attractive person. We speak of "charisma" or "great personality." We like the one who speaks eloquently and is neatly dressed. Leadership to us is often a matter of outward appearance. While these things are not sinful in themselves, and are certainly traits to be desired, they often become the most important factors in determining the spiritual leader. But, according to God Himself, the most important ingredient is internal, in the heart, not external.

Solomon

After a 40-year reign as king of Israel, David approached death. He called his son, Solomon, to him and charged him to walk in the ways of the Lord, keep His statutes and commandments and His judgments and His testimonies. God told Solomon that he needed a godly life-style through commitment to His commandments. Then He would establish his throne and kingdom (see 2 Chron. 7:17-20). Once again the example of a spiritual leader is set before us.

Leaders in the Old Testament had problems like you and I do...but what God demanded of them, He demands of us.

We could speak of many others in Israel's history and of the lessons they learned. It is easy to say that these men of the Old Testament were "super saints" and not like you and me. But James 5:17 reminds us of Elijah, the great prophet of God, who was a man "with a nature like ours." Leaders in the Old Testament had problems like you and I do. What God told them about spiritual leadership applies to us as well. We're not perfect, but neither were they. We need God's help, and so did they. What God demanded of them, He demands of us. The example of the leader is fundamental to the effectiveness of what he says and does. It is crucial to the people who must depend upon that leadership.

NEW TESTAMENT EXAMPLES OF LEADERSHIP

In the Early Church

In the New Testament, the concepts of leadership are developed from the standards set forth for elders (or bishops) and deacons. In Acts 6:1-7 we learn that because of the growth of the church ("the disciples were increasing in number") certain administrative problems demanded additional leadership help. When the apostles called the believers together to consider the problem, they challenged them to select seven men from among themselves.

The best kind of a leader is one chosen by the people he leads. He comes from their own number. They know him and have observed his life-style. Acts 6:3 says there should be a time for observing their conduct before they are selected for leadership. The words "of good reputation" refer to those who have been constantly witnessed or watched by others.

These men were to be full of the Holy Spirit, wisdom, and faith. It doesn't mean they were perfect. It means they manifested these qualities as habits of life. There should be a period of time in which the good seed of God's Word can bring forth recognizable fruit. Leaders need wisdom and faith, and that comes through experience and maturity. Without faith, there will be little growth, vision or outreach. Without wisdom, many wrong decisions will be made. Placing new converts into leadership is not wise. Their leadership traits as believers have not had enough time to develop and become obvious to others.

As a young pastor trying to start a church, I knew we needed spiritual leaders, but I wasn't sure how to go about it. A man was chosen for leadership who was a new believer. In the world's eyes, he was qualified. He was influential, wealthy and well-educated. In every way, he appeared to be successful.

Well, I learned the hard way that spiritual leaders are made over a period of time, not born! He constantly had problems with situations and people in the church. He did not understand people, and he lacked maturity in dealing with them. He did not see things from God's viewpoint but rather from the vantage point of one with worldly wisdom. He has grown much in the years that followed, and we both look back to that time with greater understanding.

Paul's Advice on Leadership

The apostle Paul knew the importance of the leader's example. He said, "The things you have learned and received and heard and seen in me, practice these things; and the God of peace shall be with you" (Phil. 4:9). In Hebrews 13:7 he wrote: "Remember those who led you, who spoke the word of God to you; and considering the result of their conduct, imitate their faith."

A classic example of Paul's advice to leaders is found in Acts 20. He called the elders of the church in Ephesus to meet with him at a place called Miletus. In that beautiful talk he continually reminded them of his own example of leadership. He wanted them to follow his steps, to do and live as he had done among them. That's the secret of good leadership—inspiring others to follow your example.

I was reminded of this important truth one day when I stopped a little boy in the hall of our Sunday School building and said, "What do you want to be when you grow up?" Without a moment's hesitation he said, "Just like my dad!" How fortunate that dad! What an honor to have your son respond like that! That little boy was so proud of his dad, and he wanted to follow his dad's example. Again, that's what real leadership is all about!

Paul said to Timothy, "And the things which you have heard from me in the presence of many witnesses, these entrust to faithful men, who will be able to teach others also" (2 Tim. 2:2). The words "from me" are literally "alongside of me." Timothy was able to observe Paul's example and to learn about leadership through what Paul did. That's the same method our Lord used. Mark 3:14 says, "And He appointed twelve, that they might be with Him." Christ gave His apostles an example to follow.

What kind of example should a spiritual leader be? All these examples show one important truth. The way a leader lives speaks so loudly that you can't always hear what he says. It is a godly life-style that makes a spiritual leader what he ought to be so others can depend upon his leadership. A leader must be obedient to God's Word and follow the example of men like Moses, Joshua, David, Paul and, of course, Jesus Christ! A leader must walk with God— be a man of prayer and be obedient to God. He must recognize that the way he lives before others is a key to his leadership. May God make us all what He wants us to be!

☑ LEADER'S CHECKLIST

1. Do you, like Moses, try to do it all by yourself?
2. Can you name someone whom you have trained to help you?
3. Is your job description like that of Moses? How is it different?
4. Are you violating a known principle of God's Word in the exercise of your leadership? In what way?
5. Is your example before others leading them to live for God? List three ways you can tell.
6. Do others have the opportunity to be with you in

order to observe your example, or do you remain aloof from people? List six ways you regularly open yourself up to others.

7. Do you really believe that the example of your life should be followed by others? Why?

2
How to Recognize a Spiritual Leader

SEVERAL years ago my faith and confidence in a certain Christian leader was shattered. I could hardly believe that he was not the spiritual leader I had always thought him to be. This caused me to ask the question I have asked many times since: "How do you recognize a spiritual leader?" How can I be sure that a person is a spiritual leader instead of just putting on an act in front of others? Let's face it—that question has troubled all of us at one time or another.

One day it dawned on me that the qualifications of 1 Timothy 3 for elders (bishops) and deacons was the answer to recognizing spiritual leaders. These qualities are not just for the select few, but represent what a godly man is really like. These are standards for everyone, and especially for leaders.

The way to select or recognize a spiritual leader is to check out his life-style with 1 Timothy 3 and see if he manifests these traits as a habit of life. Of course no one is perfect. There will be moments of weakness and failure. But the key is whether or not there is an overall pattern of life that reflects these qualities. A person could fool you at any one given moment of time, but it is quite difficult to deceive those who live with you and know you over a long period of time.

When a person is filled with the Spirit and obedient to the Word, these qualities will be reflected in that person's life. Each of these traits mentioned are important and worthy of detailed study. Any person who desires to be a spiritual leader should constantly refer to this listing in 1 Timothy 3 (also Titus 1) for guidance and direction.

Do You Desire to Be a Spiritual Leader?

First Timothy 3:1 tells us that there will be a continual desire for spiritual leadership. The Greek words used suggest an intense desire, reaching out after a goal. It isn't a momentary fancy, but rather something that stays with you. When God calls you to leadership, there is no lightning bolt in the sky or bells ringing. God plants a continual desire in your heart. No one needs to keep motivating you to leadership. You begin to experience self-motivation. Experience shows us that those who do not have a continual desire for leadership will usually fail in a crisis or give up when things get tough.

One of the young men in our church who had been placed in a position of leadership was failing to motivate others or to get people to respond to his leadership. He became deeply depressed and discouraged. He began to question his ability as a leader, and to doubt that God had called him to that role. When we finally talked about it, the root of the problem was the lack of desire in his heart for spiritual leadership. He simply did not want it. He did not want to pay the price of leadership or face the risks involved.

After some counsel, he stepped out of that role of leadership and assumed the role of following others. Happiness returned to him, and he once again had the peace of God

Leadership is not for everyone. The demands are great, and the pressures are intense.

in his life. Leadership is not for everyone. The demands are great. The pressures are so intense at times that apart from knowing God has called you, you could easily throw in the towel.

Everyone has experienced at one time or another a desire to be a leader. But, real spiritual leadership must be based upon a constant desire. You want to be a leader more than anything else! God's call is deeply impressed upon your heart and you think about it all the time. That's desire!

How Long Have You Been a Christian?

It takes maturity and experience to be a spiritual leader. First Timothy 3:9 says that deacons must be "holding to the mystery of the faith with a clear conscience." A spiritual leader must be settled in his own commitment to the gospel of Christ and the doctrines of God's Word without any hesitation. A man who doubts his relationship to Christ will not be a spiritual leader to others.

One of the men in our church was struggling with a man he led to Christ. He wanted to disciple him, but ran into many problems. The person he led to Christ began to grow and develop, and soon was more mature than the one who was to be his spiritual leader. When the situation finally came to my attention, I realized that the first man was having problems because of his own lack of security and assurance as to his relationship with Christ. It is difficult to be a spiritual leader to someone else when there is a lack of confidence in your own heart about your commitment to Christ.

First Timothy 3:6 says that one who aspires to an office of leadership should not be "a new convert, lest he become conceited and fall into the condemnation incurred by the devil." A position of leadership can easily lead to pride in the heart of the new convert. But with maturity we can see things differently and with proper attitudes. First Timothy 3:10 adds, "And let these also first be tested." The testing here is for the purpose of receiving approval. People who have been under trial and testing and have proven themselves faithful under these conditions will make the best leaders every time!

An overseer (bishop) should be "above reproach," according to 1 Timothy 3:2. The Greek word refers to a specific charge against someone. The idea of this quality in one's life is that there should be no specific charge of violating God's Word that can be brought against that person. Of course, it doesn't mean he is perfect! It means that all affairs are in order, with no loose ends such as unresolved conflicts and problems from the past. Then Paul adds, "And he must have a good reputation with those outside the church, so that he may not fall into reproach and the snare of the devil" (1 Tim. 3:7). Spiritual leaders must have a consistent testimony and life-style among nonbelievers as well as believers.

One of my friends in the ministry lost his leadership because of bad debts. He got himself into such financial trouble that his testimony and reputation were destroyed in that community and his church suffered deeply in the process.

Maturity and developing a good reputation take time. You don't become a leader in one day! Be patient while others have the chance to watch you as you grow and minister in the Body of Christ. Spiritual leadership is no place for a new believer.

Your Marriage Affects Your Leadership

What you are like in your home often reveals your right to a position of leadership. Those who know us best live with us every day. First Timothy 3:2 says that the leader must be "the husband of one wife." (See also v. 12.) There are all kinds of views about that phrase, including issues like polygamy, divorce and remarriage. Literally, the phrase reads, "a one-woman man." Devotion without question is the way I read that! There should be no doubt in people's minds about your loyalty and love for your marital partner!

My wife is my best friend. She loves me in spite of what she knows about me, and our love has deepened through the many years of our marriage. We are both thankful. She doesn't realize as much as I the importance of her life and love to my leadership.

Something would depart out of my leadership without her loving companionship and support. She's always there. I love to go home. I don't know all the joys we will experience in heaven, but the love between my wife and me has got to be close! Having said that doesn't mean we don't have problems like everyone else; we do! But we both understand the importance of our commitment and companionship to one another as it relates to spiritual leadership.

Tragedies in marriages are always hard to accept, and especially when they happen to spiritual leaders. We all know examples that have broken our hearts. Perhaps we would do ourselves a favor if we insisted on stronger evidence for marital fidelity in the lives of those we select for leadership rather than the simple fact that they are married or that they have never been divorced.

The leader's commitment and love for his marital partner reveals much about the kind of leadership he has with others. If strong love is not evident in the marriage, it may also be absent in the leader's relationships to those around him. If he is critical of his wife, he will probably be critical of those with whom he works and ministers to. Yes, your marriage does affect your leadership!

Do Your Children Respond to Your Leadership?

First Timothy 3:4,5 reveals that a man cannot really take care of the church if he can't take care of his own children. But what does that mean? Are parents responsible for the sins of their children? Ezekiel 18:20 says no. Parents are responsible for managing their children, but even under the best parental care, some children rebel (they have a sin nature too, you know) and break their parents' hearts. Still, leadership qualities are often revealed in the way a person handles his children.

First Timothy 3:4 uses the word "manage," which means literally "to stand before" others. It refers to a leader who motivates and challenges others. It refers also to training and teaching. In other words, according to this text, a spiritual leader should have a father's heart; he is to keep his children under control with all dignity; he has a certain seriousness of mind and purpose about him; he is calm, purposeful, and stable—his control is not that of a tyrant who screams and yells at his children. He manages with dignity and self-control.

Every time I got angry at what my children had done I would get this gnawing feeling inside that I just disquali-

---

A leader who is insecure will make others insecure. If he is nervous under pressure, everyone else will be also.

---

fied myself for the ministry of leadership! It usually affected me right about the time of disciplining my children. The devil wanted me to stop but I knew that discipline was necessary and that it revealed my love for them.

But attempts to discipline children can also reveal problems. Sometimes we are angry without reason other than personal inconvenience. Your children can respond to you out of fear rather than respect or love. A certain amount of godly fear is necessary, I suppose, but sometimes there is a fine line between appropriate and inappropriate fear.

Proverbs 13:24 says, "He who spares his rod hates his son, but he who loves him disciplines him diligently." But on the other side, Ephesians 6:4 says, "And, fathers, do not provoke your children to anger; but bring them up in the discipline and instruction of the Lord." How we need the wisdom of God!

It seems to me that the basic way a man's leadership is affected by his family life depends on how he deals with them in various situations. Does he apply discipline when it's needed? If he doesn't, then he will lack the courage or understanding in applying biblical discipline to believers who are not walking with the Lord. Does he talk with his children? Do they feel free to talk with him? This will obviously affect his communication with those under his leadership. Does he demonstrate love for his children, spending time with them, doing things together? If this is missing, the leader will probably be that way in his relationships with others. Again, taking care of your family is essential in order to take care of other believers.

How Do You Feel About Yourself?

Two traits are mentioned in 1 Timothy 3 that deal with your attitudes and reactions toward yourself and your abilities.

1. A leader should be temperate. A temperate person is sober and calm in judgment; clear in thinking and perspective. He is someone who is stable and does not overreact to situations, becoming overwhelmed, nervous or insecure. A leader who is insecure will make others insecure. If he is nervous under pressure, everyone else will be also.

This came to my attention as an important leadership trait when I was confronted with a serious situation and said, "What are we ever going to do?" A co-worker said, "We? You're the leader!" Suddenly I realized what temperate means. When confronted with the situation by myself I felt nervous and insecure, and wondered how in the world we could ever handle that problem. A leader must learn to be calm and to think through things from God's perspective, not man's.

2. A leader should be prudent. A prudent person has a quality of mind that is humble and sound in his evaluations of his own abilities and gifts. There are two extremes to be avoided when looking at this quality. One extreme happens when Christians see themselves as nothing. They think they are worthless. They forget what God sees. He knows our sin and weakness, but He also sees our value and worth—that's why He redeemed us! We are valuable to Him, and we belong to Him! He wants us to glorify Him in the bodies that He purchased (see 1 Cor. 6:19,20). A prudent leader is one who knows that he has value because of what God has already done in his life, and what He can do in the future.

The other extreme happens when believers have an exalted view of themselves. They ignore the grace of God and start boasting in their own abilities and talents. How sad when conceit and feelings of self-importance take over in a spiritual leader's life!

I sat in the office of a Christian leader one day, admiring the many accomplishments in his life and ministry. When I asked, "To what do you attribute your success?" he proceeded to tell me about his educational background, his talents, his way with people, his good business sense, etc. I was very disappointed. I heard nothing of the grace and power of God.

A temperate and prudent leader has his act together. He understands that the grace of God is behind his abilities. He is calm in a crisis and able to view it from the perspective of a sovereign God.

How Do You Handle Circumstances?

Things change. Nothing remains the same. Things today are changing more rapidly than ever before. Change puts pressure on us. Paul, in 1 Timothy 3:2, refers to a quality called "respectable." The Greek word comes from the word that gives us our name for the universe, *cosmos*. It refers to the arrangement of things. The English word "cosmetics" is based on it—the arrangement of things on the face!

So a respectable leader is well-arranged. His mind is organized and he does not feel swamped by life's pressures and circumstances. He thrives on them. He doesn't cop out of responsibilities, but rather he faces them head-on.

A leader's desk is often a reflection of his leadership. (Ouch! That remark hurt a little!) I guess it's OK to have your desk cluttered if you know where everything is that you need. However, to me that condition is convicting! I find that a clean desk at the end of the day (when possible) is a mark of good leadership. Don't put things off—deal with them today, if possible. You'll sleep better!

HOW DO LEADERS REACT TO PEOPLE?

Five words in 1 Timothy 3:2,3 suggest the manner in which leaders should react to people. They are: hospitable, able to teach, gentle, not pugnacious, and uncontentious.

To be hospitable means loving strangers or guests—at work as well as at home. Hospitable refers to a person who is open to people, desiring to minister in some way. Leaders who are cold and aloof do not make good spiritual leaders. We need to be warm and friendly to all.

I was reminded of this recently when a man said to me that he really liked teaching school; it was the students who bothered him!

Able to teach refers to the way we communicate. It is used only one other time in the Bible, in 2 Timothy 2:24. The context there clearly shows that this is the quality of one who presents God's Word in a nonthreatening, objective, patient and loving manner. The best way to identify this trait is when others disagree with you. If you jump all over them, condemning them or their viewpoint with great hostility (using spiritual words, of course!), then you are not manifesting the ability to teach. You yourself are not teachable. Every person is our teacher (even if we

> *You can't be a spiritual leader if you are continually fighting others, insisting on your own way and rights.*

learn what not to do!). We need to be patient and loving at all times.

To be gentle is the opposite of being quick-tempered or contentious. It refers to one who is patient and forbearing. There is a willingness to yield to the other person. Ask yourself the question, "When was the last time I gave in to another person's opinion or viewpoint?" Are you always right?

A pugnacious person is one who physically strikes another person because of loss of control. This person has an angry, violent temperament. This has no place in spiritual leadership.

We had to ask one of our leaders to step down from leadership because he physically struck his wife on more than one occasion. At first he was very defensive when confronted (often a sign of guilt), but when he knew we had the facts, he realized he had forfeited his right to leadership.

Uncontentious—you can't be a spiritual leader if you are continually fighting others, insisting on your own way and rights. Some of us do that with issues as well as people. We pound a point into the ground that others see as minor and unimportant. We fight for things that have no value except in our own eyes. A spiritual leader knows when to yield and when to stand for what's right.

All of these traits affect our relationships with people and our ability to serve as a spiritual leader. There may be weak moments when you fail in one of these; but the question is whether they are observable patterns in your life.

BAD HABITS CAN DESTROY YOUR LEADERSHIP!

Two bad habits that a leader should avoid are listed in 1 Timothy 3. God wouldn't have listed them if they were not important and serious problems.

A spiritual leader must avoid being addicted to wine. The text indicates that he is not to be "alongside of" wine. It can refer to a drunk, but drunkennesss is always a sin in the Bible. It can also refer to one who sits beside the wine when he feels the need to trust in it to solve his problems or drown his sorrows. A spiritual leader must have his confidence in the Lord and must learn to face his problems, not run away from them.

Under the guise of Christian liberty, many believers today feel free to drink alcoholic beverages. They use the Bible to justify their desire to have a little wine. After all, wine was used in Bible times. It was the Oriental beverage. The problem with all of this is that the word for "wine" can be applied to wine in its various stages of fermentation. Some passages in the Bible (such as Prov. 23:29-35) condemn the usage of wine in certain stages.

Without ignoring the medicinal usage of wine (see 1

Tim. 5:23) or the particular situations that we must face in the exercise of Christian liberty (see 1 Cor. 10:27), let's ask ourselves a basic question that is really a matter of spiritual leadership: "Why do you want to partake in that which is questionable?" Don't you have the freedom as a believer to refrain from doing that which others may do in order to be more effective in your ministry for the Lord?

Spiritual leaders should live "above reproach." Maybe you can handle it and maybe you can't. But your leadership is a higher priority than your personal desires. Why indulge (even if limited to rare occasions) in that which is questionable at all?

I asked one of our deacons who was having a problem in this area what he would think if I had a drink once in a while. He said that he would question my leadership as his pastor. How inconsistent! He had a double standard. He wanted to be a spiritual leader like his pastor, but his personal desires were getting in the way. He concluded that as a deacon it was OK, but for the pastors—No! He even used the Scriptures to prove his point, pointing out that the deacons were forbidden to take "much wine" (1 Tim. 3:8), and that meant he could have a drink or two at times.

The deacon was a close friend of mine, and the conclusion of this whole matter was that he saw his desire for wine as a hindrance to his spiritual leadership. He made a decision to get it out of his life. I have noticed a tremendous difference in his commitment to Christ ever since. It may seem like a small thing to you, but it does affect our spiritual leadership.

The second bad habit is the love of money. One without this habit has no ambition to be rich, nor is he impressed by great wealth. Money does not control his decisions. He is contented in this area (see 1 Tim. 6:6-10) and recognizes the tremendous heartaches and problems that can happen in the life of one controlled by the love of money.

One of my friends in the ministry lost his leadership over the love he had for money and what money can buy. "Things" became more important than people in his life. He always wanted a nicer car, a bigger house and a larger salary. It was embarrassing at times to talk with him because these things so dominated his conversation. I was not surprised when he left the ministry.

Recognizing a spiritual leader is the responsibility of God's people. Believers must be careful when they choose leaders. The standards of God's Word should be carefully observed. Always check a person's life over a period of time—never decide on the spur of a moment. Look for patterns, not moments of weakness. Above all, pray for God's wisdom and direction.

☑ LEADER'S CHECKLIST

1. Is there a continual desire in your heart for leadership? Describe it in a sentence or two.
2. Are you a new believer?
3. Are you devoted to your marital partner without any hesitation? Describe your feelings.
4. Do your children respond to your leadership? Why or why not?
5. Are you stable in difficult situations? Think of some recent examples.
6. Are you humble in evaluating your talents and gifts?
7. Do circumstances overwhelm you?
8. Are you patient with people or do they irritate you? List people who irritate you and try to understand why. How can you change your approach?

9. Do you yield to others or must you always be right?
10. Are you willing to give up questionable things in order to be a leader? List some pastimes, things, etc., you have either given up or are willing to give up.

3
CAN YOU BE TRUSTED?

A business magazine several years ago told the story of a London executive who purchased a new Rolls Royce. He planned a holiday in Europe and ordered his new car to be delivered to Paris. After picking it up, he started out on his trip, driving through the countryside of France. On a deserted road, much to his amazement, his new car broke down. After calling the company in England, he was told to find a place to stay (at their expense) and one of their mechanics would be sent.

When the mechanic arrived, the car was fixed in a matter of hours, and the man was on his way again. After touring Europe for several weeks, he became concerned about the potential costs involved in making the repairs. Back in England, he called the company about the possible maintenance fees, and received a letter in reply that said:

"According to our records, nothing has ever gone wrong with a Rolls Royce. There will be no charges!"

How wonderful it would be to learn of spiritual leaders in whose lives and leadership "nothing has ever gone wrong"!

Since the events of Watergate, Vietnam, television scandals among religious leaders, political corruption and financial disasters and deception on Wall Street and in leading banking institutions, Americans have become skeptical and hesitant in supporting and following our leaders. We question the veracity and reliability of persons in authority, and with the rise of the cult of the individual, we often rebel and refuse to submit to what we are told by those in positions of leadership.

IS ANYONE WITHOUT MORAL BLEMISH?

The Bible speaks of human depravity, teaching that all of us are sinners (Ps. 51:5; Rom. 3:10-12, 23), and that none of us is capable of good in the eyes of God. Proverbs 20:9 asks, "Who can say, 'I have cleansed my heart, I am pure from my sin'?" Obviously...no one! Ecclesiastes 7:20 adds: "Indeed, there is not a righteous man on earth who continually does good and who never sins."

We are warned in 1 John 1:6-10 that it is impossible to deny the presence or practice of sin in our lives. It is a reality that every mature believer understands will remain until the second coming of Jesus Christ, when we receive our glorified bodies. Only then will sin be removed from us forever.

But the gospel of Jesus Christ sets us free from the penalty and power of sin. Our position in Christ declares us righteous before God, perfect in His sight because of the death and resurrection of Jesus Christ our Lord. He paid for all of our sins—past, present and future. There is now no condemnation to those who are in Christ (Rom. 8:1), and we do not have to remain in bondage to sin (Rom. 6).

Spiritual leaders should understand that believers can live godly and righteously in this present world. We are pressured like everyone else, both from within and from without. But, through the control of the Holy Spirit (Gal. 5:16) and the cleansing power of God's Word (Ps. 119:9, 11), we can be victorious over sinful desires and temptations.

CAN WE HAVE A GODLY LIFE-STYLE IN THESE DIFFICULT DAYS?

Jesus spoke of a coming time when there would be a phenomenal rise in "lawlessness" (Matt. 24:12). Moral standards would collapse, and the spiritual commitment of the majority would continue to diminish. The apostle Paul wrote these words in his last letter before his death:

> But realize this, that in the last days difficult times will come. For men will be lovers of self, lovers of money, boastful, arrogant, revilers, disobedient to parents, ungrateful, unholy, unloving, irreconcilable, malicious gossips, without self-control, brutal, haters of good, treacherous, reckless, conceited, lovers of pleasure rather than lovers of God; holding to a form of godliness, although they have denied its power; and avoid such men as these (2 Tim. 3:1-5).

What a description of our times—"lovers of self, lovers of money" and "lovers of pleasure"!

Pursuing Moral Purity

Our secular society is dominated by a lack of moral values. Our doctrine of moral neutrality has led us into a moral mess! Freedom to do whatever we want to do has produced a weak and sick society where human life is no longer sacred, and sexual values have been reduced to the level of animal desire and lust.

The Bible teaches that we all have sexual desire, and that it is stronger in some people than in others. Those with strong sexual desire are urged to be married, and not seek sexual satisfaction outside of the bonds of matrimony (1 Cor. 7:1-9).

Our culture is filled with temptation, enticement, sexual innuendos and allurements. Our advertising and marketing styles have promoted sensuality as a great motive for financial investment and purchase. There is nowhere to hide! Sometimes it seems so futile to oppose what society is now tolerating. Because of our own weakness and vulnerability, one can become hesitant to confront sinful behavior, knowing full well that the danger of moral lapse lies within our own hearts.

But, we do not have to go along! We can say no to sinful behavior. Perhaps the strongest test of a spiritual leader's credibility and integrity is the ability to say no to that which is wrong and destructive.

IS MORAL PURITY A REQUIREMENT FOR SPIRITUAL LEADERSHIP?

The very words "moral purity" connect in some secular minds as an impossible fantasy of those characterized by self-righteous attitudes that reflect the values of a previous Victorian time rather than the values of today's ethical systems. *We* set the rules today, rather than God. We decide who is right and who is wrong. As long as no one gets hurt by what we do, then what difference does it make? That's how values and ethics are being communicated in the educational and social institutions of our present culture.

Spiritual leaders who are mature (and all of them should

be!) are well aware of the depravity of the human heart. They understand clearly how easy it is to sin against God and His standards. Their awareness of spiritual helplessness in the face of depravity and temptation causes them to depend upon God's power and not their own.

While they may sin (and do!), they do not continue to justify, defend or tolerate such behavior, either in them-

> ## *No spiritual leaders are doing the will of God if they are involved in sexual immorality.*

selves or in others. They are grateful for God's forgiveness, grace and love, and seek to reflect those wonderful attributes to others who are troubled and overwhelmed by sinful temptation and behavior.

Biblical Guidelines for Purity

Moral purity is the quality of a spiritual leader that keeps that person from continuing in known sinful behavior. Consider the following facts from the Bible:

1. Moral purity is a requirement for church leaders. In the qualifications of 1 Timothy 3:2,12, and in Titus 1:6, the apostle Paul urged that church leaders be the "husband of one wife." While divorce may affect that standard, the primary emphasis is moral purity. The Greek says "a one-woman man." The simple fact is that regardless of the temptation others may bring or the strong desire one may feel within for another person, the godly leader says no to leaving his spouse for another, and no to having sex with anyone other than his wife.

2. Moral purity is the foundation of true wisdom. We want our spiritual leaders to be wise people, but according to James 3:17, the wisdom that comes from God is "first pure." After purity is established, then the other traits of wisdom will be reflected in a person's life. Proverbs 29:2 says, "When the righteous increase, the people rejoice, but when a wicked man rules, people groan." We are in serious need of spiritual leaders who manifest a godly life-style and who are characterized by moral purity.

3. Moral purity is the will of God. One of the clearest statements on the will of God is found in 1 Thessalonians 4:1-8; and it deals with moral purity:

> Finally then, brethren, we request and exhort you in the Lord Jesus, that, as you received from us instruction as to how you ought to walk and please God (just as you actually do walk), that you may excel still more. For you know what command-ments we gave you by the authority of the Lord Jesus. For this is the will of God, your sanctifica-tion; that is, that you abstain from sexual immoral-ity; that each of you know how to possess his own vessel in sanctification and honor, not in lustful passion, like the Gentiles who do not know God; and that no man transgress and defraud his broth-er in the matter because the Lord is the avenger in all these things, just as we also told you before and solemnly warned you. For God has not called us for the purpose of impurity, but in sanctifica-tion. Consequently, he who rejects this is not rejecting man but the God who gives His Holy Spirit to you.

What a powerful and clear assessment of the will of

God! God has called us to holiness (1 Pet. 1:14-16). Our bodies have become temples of the Holy Spirit (1 Cor. 6:15-20), and we are not to defile them by sexual misconduct. Sexual desire is a precious gift of God (1 Cor. 7:7), and is to be fulfilled within the bond of marriage (1 Cor. 7:1-2). No spiritual leaders are doing the will of God in their lives if they are involved in sexual immorality!

4. *Moral purity is the commitment of one who desires to glorify God in his life.* First Corinthians 6:18-20 proclaims this strong admonition on moral purity:

> Flee immorality. Every other sin that a man commits is outside the body, but the immoral man sins against his own body. Or do you not know that your body is a temple of the Holy Spirit who is in you, whom you have from God, and that you are not your own? For you have been bought with a price: therefore glorify God in your body.

Sexual immorality does not glorify God. It is a sin which not only affects the emotional nature of humans, but also the physical body. Both sexual disease and sexual impotency are consequences of sexual immorality. Sexual vitality and strong desire are encouraged by sexual purity.

5. *Moral purity is the result of one who is obedient to God's Word.* Psalm 119:9-11 makes this point abundantly clear:

> How can a young man keep his way pure? By keeping it according to Thy Word. With all my heart I have sought Thee; do not let me wander from Thy commandments. Thy word I have treasured in my heart, that I may not sin against Thee.

Romans 6:17-19 also emphasizes the importance of God's Word in the freedom of the believer over sin's influence and control:

> But thanks be to God that though you were slaves of sin, you became obedient from the heart to that form of teaching to which you were committed, and having been freed from sin, you became slaves of righteousness. I am speaking in human terms because of the weakness of your flesh. For just as you presented your members as slaves to impurity and to lawlessness, resulting in further lawlessness, so now present your members as slaves to righteousness, resulting in sanctification.

Galatians 5:16 tells us to "walk by (by means of) the Spirit" and we will not carry out the lust of the flesh. Step-by-step obedience to the Holy Spirit is a life of obedience to what the Bible says is right and wrong. We don't make up the rules...God does!

6. Moral purity is the key to great leadership and effectiveness. In 2 Timothy 2:19-22, the apostle Paul gave instructions to his son in the faith, Timothy, about his own spiritual leadership in God's church and the standards by which he would select other leaders. He wrote:

> Nevertheless, the firm foundation of God stands, having this seal, "The Lord knows those who are His," and, "Let everyone who names the name of the Lord abstain from wickedness." Now in a large house there are not only gold and silver vessels, but also vessels of wood and of earthenware, and some to honor and some to dishonor. Therefore, if a man cleanses himself from these things, he will

be a vessel for honor, sanctified, useful to the Master, prepared for every good work. Now flee from youthful lusts, and pursue righteousness, faith, love and peace, with those who call on the Lord from a pure heart.

Spiritual Purity and the Leader

What better words could be used to describe the effective service of a spiritual leader—"a vessel for honor, sanctified, useful to the Master, prepared for every good work." The clear command of verse 22, "Flee from youthful lusts," makes it clear that moral impurity does more to hinder the effectiveness of the servant of the Lord than perhaps anything else.

Moral purity in the life of a spiritual leader is an essential part of integrity and trustworthiness. Our character is what we are before God, whereas our reputation is simply what people think we are. Our character is best seen in the dark when no one else knows what we are thinking, saying or doing. It is then that we discover the meaning of personal integrity, not the kind that sees only the opinions of others, but the kind that senses deeply its accountability to God.

John was a talented leader with great gifts and abilities. He could motivate others into action, and trust the Lord for great things. But John had a problem. His sexual desires led him into pornography, and after months of involvement, into serious sexual immorality. He refused to deal with it or to seek help. He tried to cover, justify and defend his actions. He thought that because others had a similar problem, people would understand. What he failed to realize is that not only do people understand, they also do not understand why a spiritual leader refuses to repent.

After close friends confronted John, and persistent efforts were made to persuade him to confess and forsake his sin, John lost his leadership. Today he is defeated and ashamed. According to his testimony, the problem lies in our unwillingness to repent and acknowledge our sin before God.

While we all sympathize with John's vulnerability and weakness (due to our own), we cannot endorse or tolerate his habit and life-style. Fortunately, his life has been changed, and he now manifests a degree of faithfulness to God and his family. However, he will never again have the leadership he once enjoyed. An awful price to pay for temporary pleasure!

THE NEED FOR FAITHFULNESS

The leader who can be trusted is the one who is faithful, not only in the issue of moral purity and fidelity, but in every area of his life. Paul wrote:

> Let a man regard us in this manner, as servants of Christ, and stewards of the mysteries of God. In this case, moreover, it is required of stewards that one be found trustworthy (1 Cor. 4:1,2).

Tychicus is called "the beloved brother and *faithful* minister in the Lord" by the apostle Paul (Eph. 6:21). In Colossians 4:7 he speaks of him again, saying, "our beloved brother and *faithful* servant and fellow bond-servant in the Lord." Epaphras is called "our beloved fellow bond-servant, who is a *faithful* servant of Christ on our behalf" (Col. 1:7). Onesimus is said to be "our *faithful* and beloved brother" (Col. 4:9).

In 1 Timothy 1:12, Paul referred to himself when he

wrote: "I thank Christ Jesus our Lord, who has strengthened me, because He considered me faithful, putting me into service." Again, he admonished us all on the basis of the coming resurrection of our physical bodies: "Therefore, my beloved brethren, be steadfast, immovable, always abounding in the work of the Lord, knowing that your toil is not in vain in the Lord" (1 Cor. 15:58).

In the training and development of leaders, Paul told Timothy to "entrust to *faithful* men" what he had seen and learned so that they would be able to teach others also (2 Tim. 2:2).

Faithfulness over the long haul is desperately needed in the lives of spiritual leaders. We need men and women who can be trusted, who have proven to be faithful in all matters of life and belief. Hebrews 13:7 makes this point clear when it instructs the believers: "Remember those who led you, who spoke the word of God to you; and considering the result of their conduct, imitate their faith."

Believers are to evaluate carefully the way leaders conduct their lives. Do they practice what they preach? Does their personal conduct match their public statements? May God give us all wisdom as we seek to find and follow true spiritual leaders, ones upon whom we can depend for spiritual leadership in this needy world of ours!

☑ LEADER'S CHECKLIST

1. Is it possible to be morally pure?
2. What resources do we have to maintain a godly lifestyle?
3. What do you believe is meant by the words "husband of one wife," and why do you think what you do about it?

4. How can a leader be wise in the decisions he or she makes?
5. What is the will of God for leaders?
6. Make a list of that which tempts you the most to violate God's Word, and write down what you intend to do about it.
7. What does faithfulness mean to you, and how do you think others feel about it?
8. What other issues are involved in being faithful besides that of moral and marital fidelity?
9. How have Christians in your community responded to the televangelist scandals? What lessons can be learned from these tragedies?

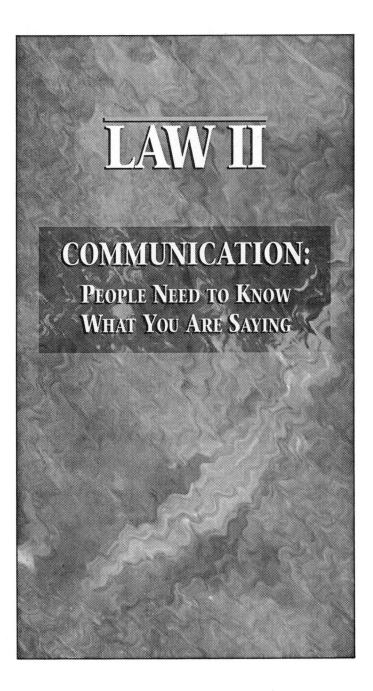

LAW II

COMMUNICATION:
PEOPLE NEED TO KNOW WHAT YOU ARE SAYING

4

YOU MUST COMMUNICATE WITH EVERYONE!

IT was a staff memo that I sent out. It was simple—just the facts. We were planning a staff retreat for a couple of days at Palm Springs. I tried to state clearly the details about place, cost, time, etc., and that the church would pay part of the cost for everyone. But I learned once again that those "inter-office memos" have a way of confusing and even irritating people! That memo was so misunderstood it resulted in several phone calls and many private conversations that consumed hours of time explaining the details that should have been clear in the memo. Oh well. You can't win them all!

COMMUNICATION: A NECESSITY, NOT A LUXURY

Communication is the name of the game! It's not an option or a creative alternative—it's an essential for good leadership! Without communication, leadership cannot exist.

Communication is not merely the ability to talk. It is not merely saying the right words at the right time. You can do all of that and still not communicate. People often

> *Leadership that does not pay attention to the importance of communication does so to its own hurt.*

read your "spirit" (attitude) more than your lips. They seem to study the way you are saying something to find out why you are saying it or how important it is.

The way people respond to your communication is often a barometer of your effectiveness in communicating. If you communicate properly, you should expect to see results. Those results should be in your mind before you start to communicate. It doesn't happen by talking a lot. Some leaders hope by their much talk that people will get the message. Ecclesiastes 5:7 says, "In many words there is emptiness."

We communicate with one another verbally and non-verbally. Even a simple glance or facial expression communicates a great deal to others. You might say that communication is a continuous process of life; life does not function apart from it. Every day and in every way we are communicating, whether good or bad. Leadership that does not pay attention to the importance of communication does so to its own hurt.

The larger the organization, the more pressing the problem of communicating with everyone becomes. Great numbers of people complicate the communication process. But if all those people are to be involved in any task or project, then each must receive communication as to what they are to do and how it is to be accomplished and when it should be done.

UNDERSTANDING LEVELS OF COMMUNICATION

In order to solve the problem of communicating to large numbers of people, organizations have designed levels of communication or responsibility. The main leader will delegate (if he is wise) responsibility to other leaders (or managers) to communicate with people under their area of responsibility. It is possible to conceive as many levels as necessary in order to limit the number of people that any one person must communicate with.

If 40 people are involved in a given task and they desire to limit the number of people to whom one person would communicate to just three people, how many levels of communication would there be? (Don't you just love riddles?) The answer: just three levels. One leader would communicate to three others on the first level (total = 4); the three leaders would each communicate to three others (total = 9); the nine would communicate to three people each (total = 27), and all 40 would get the message (you hope). That would be far more communicative than if one leader would try to reach all 39 others by himself!

Starting at the Top
Communication began with God Himself. The Father was communicating with the Son, the Son with the Spirit, etc., before the world and man were ever created. Man learned

about communication from God because God first communicated to man. He did this initially by what He made—the universe. Psalm 19:1-3 tells us that the universe is speaking all the time. It communicates to us about the greatness of God.

God also spoke directly to man in various ways (see Heb. 1:1,2) and communicated with a complete and final revelation in the Person of Jesus Christ. Today, the major way in which God is communicating to man is through the Bible.

Since the greatest communicator that ever lived is God Himself, it would be wise if the spiritual leader spent some time studying God's communication to man. Here are a few examples to get you started:

- God always spoke the truth. He never lied.
- God spoke with authority because of who He is.
- God used various methods to communicate with men.
- God told men what He wanted them to do in great detail.
- God told men what results to expect.
- God spoke with love and compassion.
- God told men why He wanted them to do what He said. It was always for their good and His glory.

The list could go on and on. We can learn much from God about how to communicate.

The Communication of Prayer

A spiritual leader will suffer greatly if he does not experience the level of communication that we call prayer—communication between man and God. There is a sense in which our communication with other people is limited when we do not communicate with God in prayer. Prayer was the first priority in Moses' job description. To talk with God is more important than talking with anyone else.

There will be times when the only way we can communicate to other people what we want to say is after prayer. There is a wonderful example of this in the book of Nehemiah. He was faced with the role of leadership; it was desperately needed due to the state of affairs in Jerusalem (see Neh. 1:2,3). The first thing Nehemiah did was to pray (see Neh. 1:4-11). When the king asked Nehemiah what his request was, Nehemiah again prayed (see Neh. 2:4). In order to communicate effectively, Nehemiah sought God's help. Do you?

Other levels of communication exist between husband and wife, parent and child, friends, at the marketplace, through TV and radio, etc. Life is filled with communication.

Leaders cannot lead effectively without communicating at all levels. You cannot isolate yourself from the people you are to lead.

THE ONE AND THE MANY

Leaders are constantly faced with the question of how to communicate between the group and the individual. Either the leader is communicating to a group of people, or a group of people are trying to communicate with the leader. The group can be a small committee of three people or a crowd of thousands. In communicating with a group, there are two basic problems. One deals with the individual's authority over the group, and the other with the group's authority over the individual. This is an extremely important matter in most organizations (including churches!).

The Key: Balance

If the individual is subservient to the group (whether committee, board or total organization), the communication problem grows, as well as the difficulties in terms of flexibility, change, implementation of ideas, etc. Many churches in America are suffering from this problem. Instead of leadership residing in the pastor, it often resides in a board

Groups do not make good leaders; individuals do! If you want someone to lead, then let him lead. Don't keep telling him how to lead!

or committee. That particular style of organization is usually a hindrance to growth. A group is incapable of making decisions quickly when needed, and communication must filter through varying viewpoints and ideas.

Our church used to be operated by the concept of a board of people representing the many ministries of the church. Communication was slow and tedious in this concept. It took much time to accomplish things. Authority moved from one person to another, and decisions were not made when needed.

After these people spent time studying the Scriptures, they changed the organizational structure and put the leadership in the hands of a few leaders, the elders, rather than in a large body of people, the board. Growth soon took place in a way the people had not seen before.

However, putting leadership in the hands of only one person can be dangerous. If that person responsible for making decisions has a bad character, then the whole organization will suffer. Proverbs 29:2 says, "When the righteous increase, the people rejoice, but when a wicked man rules, people groan." Also, if that leader does not seek the wisdom of others, whether committee or board, that organization will not succeed. Proverbs 15:22 reminds us, "With many counselors they succeed."

On the other hand, many para-church organizations have been started by individuals who, in turn, appointed a board of directors to which they had to be accountable. This in and of itself is not a bad thing, but it becomes a problem when the board is the chief decision-making instrument for the carrying on of that organization's goals.

Groups do not make good leaders; individuals do! If you want someone to lead, then let him lead. Don't keep telling him how to lead! If you don't believe he is qualified or doing the job required, then remove him and get someone who can do the job.

The key word in the relationship between an individual and a group is *balance*. The individual must recognize the importance of the group in terms of ideas, suggestions and opinions. There is importance and weight behind decisions that are recognized by a group, even though an individual made that decision. The group's role must be supportive.

The group must recognize the role of the individual as the leader. He must be free to lead. It is also wise if the leader is chosen by the group or organization. The leader will then sense overall responsibility and accountability to that group or organization. The chief role of the group is to employ the services of the leader and support him in the decisions, goals and objectives that are being carried out.

The Authority of the Leader

The frustration of being the leader but not having the authority to act was mine many years ago. I was associated with an organization whose board hired me, but placed me in the role of carrying out their decisions. I felt trapped and discouraged. I knew then and there that their system was wrong. The growth and development of the organization was hindered. The board did not face the problems on a day-to-day basis nor did they understand the needs.

HOW TO COMMUNICATE WITH A GROUP

Having faced the frustration of being a leader but not being free to lead, I have observed certain principles that affect communication between the individual and the group.

- *Establish the importance of each member of the group* in relationship to what you desire to communicate.
- *Do not reflect attitudes of superiority over the group* (in the way you talk, where you sit, how you dress or how you greet them). As a member of a board of trustees for a growing educational system I noticed how often the chairman of the board would adjust to what the other members of the board were wearing. He usually started with a suit and tie. If the board members showed up without coats, he removed his. If they had sport shirts on, he removed his coat and tie. He was a wise leader. He wanted to identify with the group to which he was communicating.
- *Maintain eye contact* with each member of the group if possible. If you don't, they will wonder why!

- *Learn to use plural pronouns,* "we" and "our," instead of singular ones, "I" and "mine." One leader irritated me and others on the committee we were serving by constantly referring to himself. As far as he was concerned, we were totally unnecessary. He definitely had an "I" problem!
- *Ask questions of members in the group,* indicating that you need their help and support. The way you ask the question is also very important. Instead of saying, "You do agree with what I'm saying, don't you?" try this one: "What do you think about it, John?" Or, "Is this the wise thing to do, in your opinion?" Or, "Is there a better way that we can do this?"
- *Allow members of the group freedom to express different ideas and opinions.* You can't really do this if you rebuke them for what they express, or if their position in the organization or their relationship with you as the leader would be jeopardized. Can others disagree with you and still be your friend?
- *Learn to admit your mistakes in the presence of the group* and to apologize sincerely when things go wrong or do not turn out the way you expected. One of the toughest assignments I have as a leader is to admit I made a mistake (especially if it's a big one!).

   I used to think that admitting you failed is a sign of weakness. It can be if you always fail! But, admitting failure in the midst of success is a key to good leadership. Learn to be open and honest before others. They'll love you for it (or at least fall over backwards out of shock!).
- *Never blame the group for the failure of the organization.* Accept the blame yourself (after all, you are the leader—ultimately, it really is your fault). A pastor once told me that the real problem in his church was his

deacons. They were the reason why his church was not growing. As long as he holds that view, his church will remain stagnant and unresponsive.

The problem is in the heart of that pastor. Instead of accepting the blame for the failure of his church to grow, he committed a "Freudian slip" by blaming others (a sure sign you're guilty of something!).

- *In small groups, call people by their first names,* unless they are very much older than you are or of higher position. In large groups, use careful discretion, especially when you do not know the person so well. It is especially tragic in communication when you cannot call someone by his right name.

  I was counseling one day with a longtime and trusted friend. In the midst of a very important sentence I called him by someone else's name. I couldn't believe I did that! Was I ever embarrassed! He felt at that moment my lack of care for him as a person. Every one of us enjoys hearing someone call our name.

- *Begin and end with prayer.* Always manifest a continual trust and dependence upon God. A group will respond to an individual better if the individual begins the conversation with prayer. In the opening prayer, ask for wisdom and guidance. In the closing prayer, express thanks and praise, regardless of the outcome.

THE ART OF CONFRONTATION

One of the more difficult forms of communication is when a group must confront an individual. This occurs in the life of a church from time to time as individuals must be confronted by two or three people, by a committee or board (see Matt. 18:15-17), or when there are organizational problems. Here are some helpful hints on handling this problem.

- *Do not isolate that person from the group in the seating arrangement.* I have never enjoyed sitting alone at the end of a table while several others sat on the other end. This will cause poor communication. Sometimes people use this seating arrangement to establish authority. That is really not necessary. It suggests an insecure authority.
- *Each member of the group should take time to greet the person, if possible.* This creates warmth immediately. The person will appreciate the concern of each member of the group to personally greet him.
- *Do not try to overpower the individual by the authority of the group.* It will be very difficult to communicate effectively if the individual believes you are trying to put him down by the importance or authority of the group. I experienced this problem once while appearing before a missions board. They continued to impress me with their authority, making me wonder whether or not my viewpoint would ever be heard. I felt on the defensive and had a difficult time communicating.

  I realize the problem was my attitude, but I also learned a lesson from that experience that I try to apply in my ministry now. A group should never try to overwhelm or impress an individual with their authority.
- *Establish the importance of the individual.* The group should do what they can to manifest their desire to hear the individual's point of view. They must be sin-

cere. The group should be willing to listen to the individual's point of view with respect.

Be careful about manifesting a critical spirit of an individual's ideas, decisions or opinions without first hearing his side. It seems that there are three sides to every issue: your view, the other person's view and the real truth. A critical spirit can cut off communication.

- *Seek to help the individual by what you say.* Prepare yourself mentally for this before the discussion ever starts. Ask yourself the question, "What can I say that will really help and build up this person?"
- *Be willing to support the individual's ideas,* unless something is morally wrong with what is said, even when those ideas may not coincide with what you were thinking. A kind word such as, "I had not thought about that," can really encourage another person. Or say something like, "I really appreciate hearing your side of this matter." Everyone likes to hear, "That's a great idea!" You may not agree with the idea, but at least acknowledge its value.
- *Do not try to communicate an idea to the individual by talking to someone else in the group.* Always look the individual in the eye and speak directly to him.
- *Seek to encourage the individual by identifying with the loneliness he feels.* So often groups fail to appreciate the position of the individual who faces the group.
- *Begin and end with prayer.*

Checking for Adequacy

One of the fundamental problems in communication is inadequate information. Everyone needs to receive communication, but often something is missing. Ask yourself,

"Does my communication tell what to do, how to do it, and when it must be done?" Be brief but be complete. Say it concisely, but make sure you've said enough.

It is hard to expect what you do not inspect. In communication, it is wise to check up on what you communicated. Do it sweetly, however. Don't make people think that you don't trust them!

One of the greatest ways to communicate with everyone is to say "thank you." A word of appreciation will greatly help your next communication. Do it personally and not in front of others. You want them to know that you are not showing appreciation just so others will think well of you. A little note from you saying "Thanks" goes a long way toward building effective communication.

☑LEADER'S CHECKLIST

1. Do you communicate daily with the Lord in prayer?
2. How many levels of communication in your ministry do you need to communicate with?
3. Are you open to people? Can they disagree with you without affecting their relationship with you?
4. Do you appreciate the viewpoints of others? How do you show it?
5. Do you look people in the eye and speak directly to them?
6. Can you apologize in front of others?
7. Do you take the blame for the failures in your organization?
8. Are you open to new ideas? Can you change your viewpoint?
9. Do you tell people "Thank you"?

5

WHAT MAKES PEOPLE LISTEN?

ONE Sunday morning after I had preached, a man came up to me in the presence of several people and began to point out what was wrong with my sermon. He did not introduce himself. I had never seen him before. He interrupted another person I was talking to. He talked quite loudly. He was angry and intolerant of others' feelings. He was judgmental without hearing the facts. He misunderstood what I said (or I misunderstood what I said!). He used bad grammar. It was time for lunch and I was hungry. My family was waiting in the car. Needless to say, we had a communication problem!

It doesn't matter what you say or how loudly you talk, some people are not listening. Communication is not one-sided. One speaks, but another must listen. Listening is a lost art. Most people are waiting for the other person to stop talking so that they can talk. Listening sometimes is nothing more than endurance! No wonder there is little communication!

I sat on the platform with a group of very distinguished people on one occasion and listened to an eloquent speaker talk for two hours to an audience of over 2,000 people. A friend of mine remarked to me afterwards that the speaker should be called "birdbath" because he was so shallow! He said nothing, but he said it well! People were obviously bored and irritated. He seemed in love with his voice and his vocabulary. *What a tragedy,* I thought.

Why People Are Not Listening

What are some of the common barriers to communication? Why do people not listen at times? What is the problem?

You Talk Too Much!

This is a very common problem. We have all met people who seem to believe that people will understand what they are trying to say if they use a lot of words. But in Ecclesiastes Solomon says, "Let your words be few" (5:2), that the "voice of a fool" comes "through many words" (5:3), and "in many words there is emptiness" (5:7).

There are two problems to face if one is talking too much. One is the problem of remembering. People listening can easily forget some of what you say because there is so much to remember! Two, one can easily become bored with a great volume of words and mentally fall asleep! (Some people do that literally!)

Many people cannot be content with sharing the important points because they sincerely believe that the "details" are what makes it interesting. Remember, *you* may think that all the details are interesting, but that doesn't mean that they are, or that they are to the person to whom you are communicating. Learn to be brief, concise and to the point. Try to state what you want to say in your first sentence. (It may save you lots of time and embarrassment!)

You Don't Say Enough

We have all had the experience of receiving some sort of communication from someone who did not give all the facts or clear enough instruction for us to do anything about what he shared. It can be very frustrating. Sometimes you wind up blaming yourself for not understanding or being able to read between the lines.

If you are a concerned communicator, you will ask questions of the people you are talking with to ascertain whether or not they have received enough information to be able to act upon what you shared.

Your Language Is Too Eloquent

We are not against good vocabulary or the right use of words in a given sentence. However, it is well known that people who try to impress others with their eloquence or style of speaking are actually putting up another barrier to communication.

The late Dr. Bob Jones, Sr., had a classic statement in this regard when he said, "It is better to say 'I seen it' than 'I saw it' if you really saw something, than to say 'I saw it' when you didn't see it at all!"

A leader will structure his message to the level of the hearer's understanding. He will take into consideration not only his audience's level of education but also their cultural background.

When we use eloquence for effect, people begin to believe that we are proud and more interested in impressing them with our vocabulary than sincerely wanting to communicate with them.

You Make Derogatory Remarks

A person can use put-downs to try to impress another person with his authority or knowledge or opinion, especially in comparison to another's point of view. We often use labels to accomplish this. We may say that a person is a "radical" and thus hope to cut off people's support of

---

People use all kinds of tricks in order to reduce the effectiveness of what someone else says or does. [This] is pride and foolish reasoning.

---

him. We may say that an issue is too "controversial" and thus avoid dealing with it. We might attack a person's views by saying, "Well, what do you expect from a man like that!" Often we question a person's motivation in the presence of others in order to diminish the importance of what that person said. It goes like this: "I know what he said, but if you really knew why he said it you would know why it is wrong."

People use all kinds of tricks in order to reduce the effectiveness of what someone else says or does. It is pride that causes it, and our foolish reasoning that believes we will look better in the eyes of others if we put people down. Ephesians 4:29 says, "Let no unwholesome word proceed from your mouth, but only such a word as is good for edification according to the need of the moment, that it may give grace to those who hear." Our desire should be to build others up, not tear them down.

You Exaggerate

People exaggerate for different reasons. Sometimes we do it to make ourselves look better than we are. Other times we do it just so people will listen to us and think that what we are saying is important. Sometimes we exaggerate in order to cover up some wrong or mistake in our lives. Very few people want to admit that exaggerations are often nothing but lies, or at least attempts to deceive people by distorting the facts. Consider the several ways we do this and recognize that they are all barriers to communication:

1. We make small incidents seem big. Some like to call this "making a mountain out of a molehill." Relationships among church members are often hurt because of this problem in communication.

Suppose one of your teenagers did not come home one night due to being stranded with automobile difficulties in another city or town. Before too long, the rumor is out that your teenager did not come home because of immorality; his reputation is destroyed by careless exaggeration of what really happened.

We have all heard examples of such stories, and have seen how they can be blown up by people who delight in relating them to others. This kind of gossip without careful knowledge of the facts is dangerous and harmful. Love does not rejoice in someone else's tragedies or problems, nor does it seek to parade them before others. Also, when you become guilty of making small incidents seem bigger than they are, you lose credibility with people and your communication is greatly affected.

2. We overgeneralize. This is a common problem among people in communication, and we must recognize how serious it is. Overgeneralizations are statements about things or people that usually contain the word "all" or "every." For example, we say, *"Everyone* knows that about him," when we *all* know that is not true! (See how I attempted to persuade you with the word "all"!)

Another example: *"Everyone* is doing it." Many young people are influenced by that kind of logic! The fact is, everyone is not doing it. The use of "everyone" is an exaggeration used by people to get others to agree with them about what they are saying.

Another example: *"Everything* has gone wrong today." Maybe a great deal has gone wrong from your perspective, but others may not feel the same way about it. We often try to make people accept our viewpoint of things by such over-generalizations. Eventually it will catch up with us, and people who think for themselves will begin to question our trustworthiness as communicators.

3. We make unfounded cause-effect statements. We use these *all* the time (there I go again!), or at least we seem to use them a great deal. In theology, we might illustrate with this statement: "Calvinism leads to dead orthodoxy," or "Arminianism leads to liberalism." Neither statement is a true cause-effect statement, even though both might be true in some cases.

Or we say, "Where there's smoke, there's fire." That little saying is often used to prove a point about someone's actions. If they do one thing, we figure automatically that they are going to do another. This is dangerous reasoning and bad communication.

"All charismatics are very emotional people." The idea here is that if you become a charismatic (theologically) you will become more emotional than if you were not one. However, there are many non-charismatics who are very emotional people, and many charismatics who seem to be unemotional and more academic and intellectual in their personality traits. Again, the cause and effect exaggeration is used by people to prove a point that they personally believe, but which cannot be established by facts.

4. *We think only in terms of either/or.* Everything seems black or white to those who use this type of reasoning. Something is either right or it is wrong. A person is either a friend or an enemy. The trouble is that life is not that simple. There are "grey areas" and "twilight zones" where we simply cannot draw such hard and fast conclusions.

We might say, "You're either a Calvinist or an Arminian—which are you?" If the person answers, "Well I think I'm somewhere in between—like a Calminian!" then we who like things black or white will become critical and judgmental of this answer and probably accuse the person of being a "compromiser."

People who aspire to be leaders must be very careful about communicating this kind of attitude. You will convince people around you that they must be 100 percent for you or they are 100 percent against you. But the truth may be that they are 90 percent for you, but 10 percent of the time they disagree with you. A wise leader allows for more flexibility than to make exaggerated either/or statements.

5. *We misuse statistics.* You have heard it said, "Figures don't lie, but liars figure!" Many of us in areas of spiritual leadership are all too aware of this problem. Statistics are used by people to prove whether or not their efforts are being mightily used of God. However, it is relatively easy to distort the facts a little without lying.

A simple example is in the use of graphs—is it vertical or horizontal? What are the numbers on the graph with which you are comparing your statistics? For instance: A graph that has divisions of 10 (like 10, 20, 30, etc.) can show a greater growth than one with divisions of 100 (like 100, 200, 300, etc.).

Also, when we use statistics, we often speak of the "average." But, what is "average"? What does that mean? Often the problem deals with what is not evident in the statistics. It is not so much what we show, but what we don't show.

A church might argue that 50 percent of a certain Sunday School class is involved in evangelism. That is all good and impressive. But suppose the class that is chosen is the smallest in numbers, and there are 20 classes that have larger attendance. And, suppose that when the church evaluates all of the classes, less than 5 percent are involved in evangelism!

The question behind the use of statistics is why the information is being shared. Is it to impress or to inform? Is it to be proud of what was accomplished or to be motivated to do better? A church may state that it had 100 decisions last year, but may fail to mention that only two of those are now members of the church and growing in their faith.

It is very easy to exaggerate a situation with the use of statistics, and leaders must be careful here in terms of their communication with people. If the facts are distorted or if the complete picture is not given, people will begin to question your motivations.

You Misuse Authorities

A very common barrier to communication is appealing to some authority (rather than God or the Scriptures) in order to substantiate what we are saying or our right to say it. When we study the reasons why people believe anything, we usually discover three sources are involved: direct experience, reasoning with certain facts or acceptance of authority.

However, when an appeal to some authority is used to prove a point or increase the chances that what the speaker says is reliable, we need to ask certain basic questions, such as, "Is the authority competent in that subject?" Or, "Is the authority reliable?" We must also ask, "Is that authority supported by other reliable sources?" We must determine how that quoted authority was supporting his point. We must ask, "What was the context of that remark?" and, "Is the authority prejudiced in that area?"

It is easy to use the appeal to authority, especially if that authority is dead! No one wants to question the reliability of some person who lived and died in a previous era and whose name represents solid Christian leadership or dedication in the past. But remember, people are people! Great leaders and authorities in the past also had certain problems and hang-ups. We must be very discerning in our use of authority.

Some of us are compulsive name-droppers. We think that by mentioning certain famous people we are substantiating the validity of our remarks. The truth may be that we are causing people to wonder why we do that. The over-use of authority often becomes a serious barrier in communication.

You Beg the Question
Simply stated, this means that we assume truth or error without proof. Leaders (sometimes because of their position) will do this often because they are used to being the authority.

Sometimes we beg the question by arguing in circles. An example of such reasoning is in the argument for evolution. A person may ask, "How do we know how old the fossils are in this particular stratum?" The answer might be, "By the stratum in which they appear." Then, you might ask, "But how do we know how old the stratum is?"

Answer: "By the fossils that appear in it." Obviously, this is "reasoning in a circle."

The common problem is that we assume the truth of a proposition that "everybody" seems to know or at least accept (for one reason or another). We sometimes use emotional words in our sentences to emphasize our point, even though we have no proof of what we are saying—statements such as, "I *really* believe this with *all my heart.*" It is commendable that you believe something that strongly, but you could possibly be wrong! Be sure the facts are clear.

All of these barriers to communication are experienced by people who work together day after day. It will help your relationships with others when you recognize what they are and learn to avoid them.

WHY PEOPLE LISTEN

It's one thing to talk about the problems, and quite another thing to have solutions! What kind of qualities make others listen to your communication? In my experience, there are at least five major qualities that are necessary for effective communication to take place.

You Are Consistently Honest
You must be honest and be able to tell the truth at all times. Sometimes it is not appropriate or necessary to reveal all that we know, but we should never lie. Sometimes we have to say, "I'm sorry, but I am not able to share that information at this time." Breakdowns in communication happen when there is a lack of honesty.

Proverbs 14:25 says, "A truthful witness saves lives, but he who speaks lies is treacherous." Verse 5 of the same chapter states, "A faithful witness will not lie, but a false witness speaks lies." Proverbs 12:19 adds, "Truthful lips will be established forever, but a lying tongue is only for a moment."

A lady shared with me the difficulty she and her husband were having in communicating with each other. It all started when she learned that he had lied to her about a certain matter. She could no longer trust him. His confes-

Effective communication is based upon the ability to listen. If people do not believe you listen to them, your leadership will diminish in their eyes.

sion to her was not complete, and so once again, she did not trust him. It was hard to listen to him. She found it difficult to talk to him under any circumstances. His lack of honesty led him to the inability to communicate effectively.

You Respect Confidences
Information that is shared in confidence must be kept that way. Leadership will diminish in the eyes of others when it is guilty of gossip. Proverbs 11:13 says, "He who goes about as a talebearer reveals secrets, but he who is trustworthy conceals a matter." Proverbs 17:9 adds, "He who covers a transgression seeks love, but he who repeats a matter separates intimate friends."

But how do you handle a situation where someone tells you to keep this in strict confidence and tell no one else? First of all, do not promise it unless you intend to keep that confidence. On certain occasions it might be better to say, "I will do my best to keep it, but I must first hear what it is to determine whether anyone else should know about it. I do promise to tell you if there is someone else who should know about this." This is important in counseling. What is shared must be told to another party if that party is involved and reconciliation is needed.

Secondly, you must determine whether what a person is going to share with you is gossip or not. Not only should we not gossip ourselves, but we should not get into the habit of listening to someone else who is gossiping. Be careful what you share with others!

You Are Open

If people are going to respond to us in personal communication, they must see an openness about us that allows them to share without fear of what we may think, say or do. Many subordinates will not share with those in authority over them because they believe they will suffer in the process.

One of our staff members was involved in a matter that necessitated his telling me about it. He kept it from me for some time until I found out about it from someone else. When I confronted him with it, he said that he didn't want to tell me about it because he thought it would affect his job. Now, that can be his problem as well as mine. It reminded me of the importance of openness. I must be open enough to fellow staff members so that they will feel free to discuss things with me without fear.

Effective communication is based upon the ability to listen. If people do not believe you listen to them, your leadership will diminish in their eyes. A part of the way in which people will evaluate this is by how many of their ideas and suggestions you eventually use. When a leader never uses any idea or suggestion someone else makes, or if he criticizes another person, people will visualize that leader as being closed and overconfident and worst of all, self-centered.

You Accept Others

People must believe that you accept them fully and unconditionally. A lack of acceptance is evident when you talk down to a person and when you are judgmental of what a person has said or done, especially when you are not involved in the situation. Often, we give our opinions when they are not wanted or needed—an unwise practice.

When you show partiality, people sense that you do not accept them. God regards us all alike, and we should so regard others.

In a counseling situation I found a man extremely hesitant about discussing his problems, even though that was his original purpose in coming to see me. He grew up in a home where the parents accepted him on the basis of how he performed. He became reluctant to share his problems lest people refuse to accept him when he wasn't performing as they expected. What a joy to tell him of God's unconditional love and total acceptance!

You Show Love

More about this in a later chapter. Just one thing at this point about love and communication: if people do not believe that you sincerely love them or care about them as people, very little real communication will take place. There will be lots of talk, but very little communication!

Paul wrote: "If I speak with the tongues of men and of angels [that's communication!], but do not have love, I have become a noisy gong or a clanging cymbal [that's noise!]" (1 Cor. 13:1). Love will deepen the level of communication. Love enriches the response of the listener. Love sweetens the way things are said. Above all, we must love!

Leadership is not so much the ability you have as an individual to do great things by yourself as it is your ability to get others to help you accomplish things. This takes good communication on a one-to-one basis. Talking with individuals before making crucial decisions is not only advisable but necessary for good leadership. Do not pull things on people without consulting with them privately. No surprises, please! We have seen that Proverbs 15:22 says, "Without consultation, plans are frustrated, but with many counselors they succeed." Amen! Let's communicate!

☑ LEADER'S CHECKLIST

(One way to answer these questions is on a scale of 1 to 10. Score yourself, then ask a trusted friend or colleague to score you.)

1. Do you talk too much, irritating people?
2. Do you say enough to tell people what to do, how to do it and when it should be done?
3. Are you conscious of being eloquent, thinking that this will impress people?
4. Do you use derogatory remarks, putting people down in order to inflate your own importance?
5. Do you have a problem with exaggerations, trying to embellish things so people will respond better?
6. Do you make too much of small incidents?
7. Do you often appeal to others in authority to make people believe what you are saying?
8. Do you assume the truth of your statements without proving them?

9. Are you known as being a truthful person at all times?
10. Do you have a problem with gossip, or can you be trusted to keep secrets in confidence?
11. Do people feel free to talk with you without fear of what you may think, say or do?
12. Do people believe that you accept and love them without conditions of performance on their part?

6

Actions Speak Louder Than Words!

TALK is easy...conduct is something else! Although many leaders do not understand this fact, *the way* something is said is often just as important as *what* is said. How a person backs up what he says by how he lives is a powerful indicator of his true leadership before others. People are not as easily fooled as we think. Just because a person has a position of authority and is called a leader does not mean that people will follow him.

LEARNING TO LISTEN—THE HARD WAY

Tom reflects great confidence in his leadership. His Christian organization has grown from just two co-workers to over 20 now. The blessing of God has been evident, donor dollars have been increasing, and the work they do has been growing in its influence and results. Lately, however, Tom has noticed a growing discontent among his workers in the office. He has not always shown great concern for office workers, but he has always given vision and challenge to them.

The problem began when Tom's habit of ignoring people's feelings started to be more noticed now that more

---

*When people believe that
you are not satisfied or contented
with your ministry unless there are
immediate results, your leadership
will weaken.*

---

people were involved in working together. It was hard for co-workers to explain this to Tom, since he was the founder and leader. He expected a great deal from those who worked for him, but rarely showed his personal appreciation. Oh, he was gracious at the annual Christmas staff occasion when awards were given. But in the daily routine of the office, workers were seldom noticed, appreciated or told that they were doing a good job.

Finally, Tom's personal secretary decided to confront him. It wasn't easy, since Tom intimidates those who work for him and under him. She began with these words: "What have I ever done for you that makes you thankful to have me as your secretary?" The question startled him. "Why did you say that?" he asked.

The secretary proceeded to tell Tom that in the three

years she had worked for him he had never shown any personal appreciation for what she had done for him. She made it clear that she was working for the Lord, and that she would continue regardless of any change on his part, but that she felt he needed to know not only how she felt, but how others in the office were feeling as well.

Fortunately for Tom, he listened, and the atmosphere in the office immediately changed. Today, he makes a list of things he appreciates, and seeks to compliment each person with whom he has contact. A simple thing...but an important insight!

THE COMMUNICATOR AS A LISTENER

Leadership demands good communication, and good communication depends upon the ability to listen, as well as to show appreciation, as in Tom's case. The action of listening to people is a part of communicating with them. In turn, the willingness to listen is rooted in several things:

1. The desire of the listener.
2. The content that is being communicated.
3. The ability of the communicator.
4. The attitudes of the communicator.
5. The respect and appreciation of the communicator by the listener.

Getting people to listen depends on the communicator's behavior much more than most communicators want to admit. A given subject can be very attractive and interesting to the listener, but be poorly received because of the attitudes, character or past conduct of the communicator.

PROBLEMS CHRISTIANS HAVE WITH LEADERSHIP

Most Christian organizations realize that dealing with Christians is different from life in the secular marketplace. Because of our relationship to Jesus Christ, we are all brothers and sisters in the Lord, and we bear heavy responsibilities to one another because of it.

Christians react differently from non-Christians in certain respects, although some basics of communication affect both groups. Christians who know what the Bible teaches about attitudes and life-styles will have a tendency to rate these matters far higher than the abilities and skills of the communicator. For Christians, actions do indeed speak louder than words!

In order for us to understand how our actions and attitudes are affecting our communication with others, it is important to see how Christians respond to the behavior they see in a leader. Negatively, it is helpful to analyze what Christians resent in the behavior of a leader. Such conduct can seriously damage the way our leadership is perceived and received.

Sacrificing the Permanent for the Immediate

People often believe that the leader wants instant success and is not willing to wait for it in God's plan and timing. The "get-rich-quick" mentality has unfortunately crept into Christian churches and organizations. The average length of time for pastors to stay in one local church suggests that unless change, progress or growth occurs quickly, we will move on to "greener pastures." The apostle Paul wrote these words to the younger minister Timothy:

> Until I come, give attention to the public reading of Scripture, to exhortation and teaching. Do not

neglect the spiritual gift within you, which was bestowed upon you through prophetic utterance with the laying on of hands by the presbytery. Take pains with these things; be absorbed in them, so that your progress may be evident to all. Pay close attention to yourself and to your teaching; persevere in these things; for as you do this you will insure salvation both for yourself and for those who hear you (1 Tim. 4:13-16).

The admonition to "persevere in these things" implies a concern for the long haul, not the short-term results that do not last. In Paul's last epistle to Timothy, he wrote:

But you, be sober in all things, endure hardship, do the work of an evangelist, fulfill your ministry. For I am already being poured out as a drink offering, and the time of my departure has come. I have fought the good fight, I have finished the course, I have kept the faith; in the future there is laid up for me the crown of righteousness, which the Lord, the righteous Judge, will award to me on that day; and not only to me, but also to all who have loved His appearing (2 Tim. 4:5-8).

Paul's words "fulfill your ministry" require a deep concern for long-range results, not short-term ones. Paul said, "I have finished the course." He had completed what God had in mind for Paul's life and ministry when He saved him.

When people believe that you are not satisfied or contented with your ministry unless there are immediate results, your leadership will weaken. Leaders need to be there, faithfully fulfilling their responsibilities, even when things are not as productive as they once were or as people hoped they would be.

Strong disciples are not made in a few months...it takes years. The rapidity of change is causing all of us to demand quicker results. We show great unhappiness over ministries and methods that are not as productive as we think they should be.

What is the problem? The problem in the leader that causes the sacrifice of the permanent, long-range result for the immediate one is the problem of *impatience.* This may reflect itself in terms of ministering to people or in how one evaluates the statistics of the ministry.

James helps us to understand our need of patience:

> Consider it all joy, my brethren, when you en-
> counter various trials, knowing that the testing of
> your faith produces endurance. And let endurance
> have its perfect result, that you may be perfect and
> complete, lacking in nothing (James 1:2-4).

Again James exhorts us about patience:

> Be patient, therefore, brethren, until the coming
> of the Lord. Behold, the farmer waits for the pre-
> cious produce of the soil, being patient about it,
> until it gets the early and late rains. You too be
> patient; strengthen your hearts, for the coming of
> the Lord is at hand. Do not complain, brethren,
> against one another, that you yourselves may not
> be judged; behold, the Judge is standing right at
> the door. As an example, brethren, of suffering
> and patience, take the prophets who spoke in the
> name of the Lord. Behold, we count those blessed
> who endured. You have heard of the endurance
> of Job and have seen the outcome of the Lord's

dealings, that the Lord is full of compassion and is merciful (5:7-11).

Leaders need patience. We must often endure the lack of results, and the struggles of people who try to put into practice what we preach and teach. They will not always see what you see, nor understand what you understand. They will not always perform as you want, nor achieve the results that you believe could have been achieved.

If you want people to follow your leadership, then do not sacrifice permanent, long-range goals and results for immediate ones.

Substituting Busyness for Spiritual Growth

Mere activity and busyness are not acceptable substitutes for true spiritual growth. When people believe that we are focusing on the external rather than the internal, they become hesitant in responding to our leadership.

Christians understand that the "outer man is decaying" but that "our inner man is being renewed day by day" (2 Cor. 4:16). And during the selection process that would lead to God's choice of the shepherd boy, David, to become king of Israel, Samuel was told that "God sees not as man sees, for man looks at the outward appearance, but the Lord looks at the heart" (1 Sam.16:7).

Busyness can lead to spiritual barrenness. Doing lots of things does not necessarily lead to great spiritual growth. In Luke 10:38-42 we read an insightful analysis of this problem:

> Now as they were traveling along, He entered a certain village; and a woman named Martha welcomed Him into her home. And she had a sister called Mary, who moreover was listening to the

Lord's word, seated at His feet. But Martha was distracted with all her preparations; and she came up to Him, and said, "Lord, do You not care that my sister has left me to do all the serving alone? Then tell her to help me." But the Lord answered and said to her, "Martha, Martha, you are worried and bothered about so many things; but only a few things are necessary, really only one, for Mary has chosen the good part, which shall not be taken away from her."

Later, in John 12:2, another meal was served in Bethany, and Martha was serving again. But this time, there was no struggle, and no loving rebuke from the Lord. The problem lies not in the serving, but in our attitude toward this activity when compared with true spiritual growth. People who are growing in the Lord are not bothered as Martha was.

Much of what we call "church work" is in the arena of busyness. People can do things for years without ever spending time with the Lord and learning from Him at His feet. Our service for the Lord becomes so much more enjoyable and effective when we are personally growing in our relationship with Jesus Christ.

What is the problem? The problem here is *immaturity*, even though leaders find it difficult to acknowledge. The immaturity lies in the leader's evaluation of what is really important. Things do need to get done, but not at the expense of a person's growth in the Lord.

One lady, who is very busy doing things for the church and at the church property, finds it easy to excuse and defend her lack of church service attendance on the basis of all the time she spends in "doing things" that need to be done. When confronted about the need for personal growth in the Lord and through the study of His Word, she becomes very defensive and upset. She attends no Bible studies, Sunday School classes or church services, and simply responds, "I have no time for that!"

Seeking the Praise of Others over God's

Proverbs 27:2 warns, "Let another praise you, and not your own mouth; a stranger, and not your own lips." Our Christian world is filled with self-promotion. Brochures, books, magazines, etc., proclaim the talents, virtues and accomplishments of religious personalities, all with an effort to influence people's response and cooperation. It is dangerous business! This is especially true when the copy that is printed in these publications has been designed by the person being promoted!

Many leaders are too careful in what they say and do, because they do not want to offend either supporters or influential people who can further their work and ministry. We seem obsessed with the approval of men, rather than the approval of God. We are intense in our efforts to get people to like us, in spite of what Jesus said:

> If the world hates you, you know that it has hated Me before it hated you. If you were of the world, the world would love its own; but because you are not of the world, but I chose you out of the world, therefore the world hates you. Remember the word that I said to you, "A slave is not greater than his master." If they persecuted Me, they will also persecute you; if they kept My word, they will keep yours also. But all these things they will do to you for My name's sake, because they do not know the One who sent Me (John 15:18-21).

Religious leaders should expect criticism and hostility from the world. Compromising our convictions in order to please men is the surest way to lose the spiritual leadership that God uses and empowers. Second Timothy 2:15 says: "Be diligent to present yourself approved to God as a workman who does not need to be ashamed, handling accurately the word of truth."

We need the approval of God, not the approval of men! In order to get God's approval, we need diligence, hard work and accurate handling of the Word of God, the Bible. Paul warns of a time that will come when the approval of men will be more important than the approval of God:

> I solemnly charge you in the presence of God and of Christ Jesus, who is to judge the living and the dead, and by His appearing and His kingdom: preach the word; be ready in season and out of season; reprove, rebuke, exhort, with great patience and instruction. For the time will come when they will not endure sound doctrine; but wanting to have their ears tickled, they will accumulate for themselves teachers in accordance to their own desires; and will turn away their ears from the truth, and will turn aside to myths (2 Tim. 4:1-4).

Much of the preaching and teaching of this culture focuses on trying to please people, rather than God. We avoid negative subjects, and speak little of repentance and consequences. There is little church discipline of habitual sinful behavior, and a great deal of unwillingness to confront wrong-doing.

When the pastor of a northwest church tried to convince his people to get involved in a citywide effort, his communication was falling on deaf ears. He could not understand his congregation's reluctance. It seems that the pastor was looking to have his name in the lights. He was already reading his press clippings too much, and his people were tired of it. They felt used and abused, and now were expressing their disapproval.

The citywide effort, in their minds, had one purpose—the further promotion of their pastor. His communication was not effective. No matter what he tried to say, people saw things differently. They were tired of how he constantly promoted himself and sought high position and words of praise from others. His awards and achievements were no longer impressing the people with whom he was to minister each week.

It was not surprising to learn of his soon departure from that ministry. If he had not resigned, the congregation would have insisted on his resignation in a matter of time.

What is the problem? The problem in the life of a leader who seeks the approval and praise of men rather than the approval of God is *indifference*—a failure to see the importance of eternal values and rewards rather than earthly honors and praise. Second Corinthians 4:17-18 puts it clearly:

> For momentary, light affliction is producing for us an eternal weight of glory far beyond all comparison, while we look not at the things which are seen, but at the things which are not seen; for the things which are seen are temporal, but the things which are not seen are eternal.

Serving for Personal Profit

Leadership in ministry is to be for the glory of God, not personal profit. Paul admonishes us all: "Whether, then, you eat or drink or whatever you do, do all to the glory of

God" (1 Cor. 10:31). Psalm 115:1 says, "Not to us, O Lord, not to us, but to Thy name give glory." The glory of God is the highest motive of Christian service!

When spiritual leaders who plead with God's people to give sacrificially to various ministries and mission endeavors are then exposed for their extravagance and huge salaries with enormous "extras" and personal benefits, no wonder people lose confidence, decrease their support or end it altogether...and rightly so!

After a radio rally in British Columbia a few years ago, a well-dressed businessman approached me with this comment: "What hotel are you using while you are staying here?" I answered quickly. He then asked how much I paid for airline tickets and whether I traveled first class. I indicated that because of my height I would love to ride in first class, but because of my pocketbook, I chose to ride in coach.

He was astonished to learn of how small our expenses were, and wondered if I was telling him the truth. I insisted that I was, and said that I would be happy to verify any and all information about it. He then proceeded to tell me about another ministry which he had supported until he learned of the extravagant expenses which that ministry incurred when holding meetings in various cities.

That gentleman was a large supporter of Christian ministries, but had a growing concern over the way financial matters were being handled. He told me of the salary levels of key leaders of organizations he was supporting and inquired about my own. He was surprised and encouraged.

That incident has been repeated many times in my presence over the past few years. God's people are becoming increasingly concerned over the personal profit and benefits many leaders are accumulating in their work for the Lord. Paul wrote in 1 Timothy 6:6-11:

> But godliness actually is a means of great gain, when accompanied by contentment. For we have brought nothing into the world, so we cannot take anything out of it either. And if we have food and covering, with these we shall be content. But those who want to get rich fall into temptation and a snare and many foolish and harmful desires which plunge men into ruin and destruction. For the love of money is a root of all sorts of evil, and some by longing for it have wandered away from the faith, and pierced themselves with many a pang. But flee from these things, you man of God; and pursue righteousness, godliness, faith, love, perseverance and gentleness.

Many leaders have destroyed their ministries and testimonies by the love of money. The desire to be rich and to have great influence because of it will lead us into many troubles, and away from true spiritual leadership.

A leader can try to motivate a group of Christians to give money to a needy cause, but if the audience perceives that the leader will personally profit greatly from the project, his communication will become ineffective. Actions speak louder than words. If the leader does not sacrifice, how can he expect the people to do so?

What is the problem? The problem here is *insincerity—* a lack of proper motives. In the example of Paul in Philippians 4:11-13 we have a great example to follow:

> Not that I speak from want; for I have learned to be content in whatever circumstances I am. I know how to get along with humble means, and I also know how to live in prosperity; in any and every circumstance I have learned the secret of being

filled and going hungry, both of having abundance and suffering need. I can do all things through Him who strengthens me.

What tremendous insights for us as we seek to be the spiritual leaders that God wants us to be! A quick summary:

1. Be content no matter what you have or don't have.
2. Trust God to meet your needs.
3. Be grateful for the help of others.
4. Give all the glory to God.

When a leader seeks personal profit rather than the glory of God, people stop listening.

A Harsh and Bitter Attitude

Speaking harshly and bitterly to people rather than kindly and lovingly can severely damage effective leadership. The fact that actions do speak louder than words is nowhere truer than here! You can say all the right things, but if your attitude is wrong, people have a hard time responding and even listening.

Bob had a heart for the Lord and His work, but a problem with attitude. He came from the streets, and grew up in a bad environment with little help from parents or family. His parents divorced when he was a small child, and when his mother remarried, his experience with his stepfather was anything but pleasant. His stepfather beat him often, and Bob finally left home.

After his conversion to Jesus Christ during the last year of his college experience, Bob felt called to the ministry. He was aggressive and enthusiastic and was a big hit among teachers and students at the seminary where he attended.

Bob was quickly offered a great opportunity to be the

senior pastor of a growing church in a metropolitan area similar to Bob's childhood experiences. It seemed to be a perfect match, and Bob's early ministry in that church was blessed. The church grew in numbers and influence, and Bob was an outspoken leader in his community for a multitude of causes.

But Bob's attitudes were not good. He often insisted on his own way. Frequently he hurt others around him who wanted to help him accomplish great things for God. He spoke in harsh tones, and people feared ever disagreeing with him. They knew that he could be very caustic and critical.

Bob seemed gifted as an evangelist, but some of his efforts were not being well-received because of the attitudes he was reflecting. He manifested a superiority complex and an arrogant spirit, especially when confronting nonbelievers. Believing friends felt it as well. His ministry, which had great potential, was beginning to suffer. Bob blamed it on others, but the problem was the way he spoke to people.

Paul gave the following advice to his young disciple, Timothy:

> And the Lord's bond-servant must not be quarrelsome, but be kind to all, able to teach, patient when wronged, with gentleness correcting those who are in opposition, if perhaps God may grant them repentance leading to the knowledge of the truth, and they may come to their senses and escape from the snare of the devil, having been held captive by him to do his will (2 Tim. 2:24-26).

When people oppose you, it is quite natural to resist them, and their arguments as well. Paul's advice—don't quarrel! Kindness and patience are needed. A gentle, non-combative attitude will help greatly when confronting the opposition.

In Hebrews 5:1-2 we read of the ideal high priest:

> For every high priest taken from among men is appointed on behalf of men in things pertaining to God, in order to offer both gifts and sacrifices for sins; he can deal gently with the ignorant and misguided, since he himself also is beset with weakness.

God expects leaders to "deal gently with the ignorant and misguided," not harshly and bitterly. Leaders are warned about their own weaknesses. Paul makes a similar point in this instruction about confronting a brother who has fallen into sin: "Brethren, even if a man is caught in any trespass, you who are spiritual, restore such a one in a spirit of gentleness; each one looking to yourself, lest you too be tempted" (Gal. 6:1).

Gentleness (meekness) is the opposite of revenge. The spirit of the person seeking to help a fallen brother is extremely important in the restorative process.

What is the problem? The problem is *insensitivity* to the needs and feelings of others. Leaders must care about those for whom they are responsible. They must genuinely desire to lead and motivate them. People will follow spiritual leaders who are keenly aware of their accountability before God in caring for others:

> Obey your leaders, and submit to them; for they keep watch over your souls, as those who will give an account. Let them do this with joy and not

with grief, for this would be unprofitable for you
(Heb.13:17).

But if we do not have kindness and gentleness in our
words, our communication will be poorly received. What
we say may be right, but the way we say it will hurt rather
than help.

A SUMMARY—ACTIONS SPEAK LOUDER THAN WORDS!

The following issues affect deeply the spiritual leader's
communication:

The Action that Hurts	The Problem that Exists
Sacrificing permanent, long-range results for immediate ones.	IMPATIENCE with people and results.
Substituting busyness and activity for true spiritual growth.	IMMATURITY in evaluating what is really important.
Seeking the praise and approval of men rather than the approval of God.	INDIFFERENCE to eternal values and reward.
Serving for personal profit, rather than the glory of God.	INSINCERITY in your motives.
Speaking harshly and bitterly to people, rather than kindly and lovingly.	INSENSITIVITY to the needs of others.

☑ LEADER'S CHECKLIST

1. What are your long-range goals, and how did you arrive at them?
2. What examples would you give to others of your impatience?
3. How would you describe true spiritual growth?
4. What activities could you eliminate in your life to make you more effective in your walk with the Lord?
5. In order to avoid criticism, what could you change about how you are promoted or advertised to others?
6. How do you identify that which glorifies God in your ministry and leadership?
7. Do you personally profit from the ministry you urge others to support? What guidelines should you have to keep yourself from wrong motives?
8. How would others describe the way you speak with them?
9. What changes could you make to improve the kindness and gentleness of your communication with others?

LAW III

ABILITY:

You Need to Be Capable of Leading Other People

7

ARE YOU ONE OF CHRIST'S GIFTED LEADERS?

WHAT kind of leaders do we need for the church today? Jesus is no longer here, but in heaven. He is building His church. He knows it needs leadership, so He designed four types of leaders. They are mentioned in Ephesians 4:11: apostles, prophets, evangelists and pastor-teachers. Ephesians 4:7 calls these leadership qualities gifts.

THE GIFTS OF LEADERSHIP

Is it possible that after studying management principles and leadership techniques, learning everything there is to know, you might still fail in being a good leader? Of course! But why? Lots of reasons. One big one might deal with spiritual gifts. The question is: Are you one of Christ's gifted leaders to the church? And: How do you know if you are one?

Let's begin by asking what these gifted leaders are supposed to do. The Bible states in Ephesians 4:12 that the four kinds of leadership here are for "equipping of the saints for the work of service, to the building up of the body of Christ." Simple enough. But what does that mean?

Equipping someone can be illustrated from the world of fishing. When fishermen in Bible times were mending their nets, the word "equipping" was used. The nets were tied together so that the fish would not slip out. The term was also used when two pieces of material were joined together. Equipping means that you are putting people together so that they can do a great work.

Second Timothy 3:16,17 tells us that the Scriptures are designed to equip the man of God for every good work. Each believer can help to build up the Body of Christ (other believers) when he is equipped. He becomes equipped with the Scriptures.

The work that the believers do in order to build up others is called the "work of service." First Peter 4:10,11 seems to indicate that this refers to the use of spiritual gifts. Every believer has at least one spiritual gift. In order to use it properly and effectively, he needs to be equipped with the knowledge of the Word of God. That assignment was given to the four gifted leaders of Ephesians 4:11. They are responsible to equip. The result will be that the Body of Christ will be built quantitatively, as well as qualitatively.

Many Christian leaders are frustrated in their jobs because they are doing things that do not reflect the kind of person God designed them to be. In other words, instead of working in the area of their gifts, they are trying to do things they were never equipped to do.

If you are presently serving as a leader in the ministry of the church, which one of the four gifted leaders are you? Are you an apostle? Prophet? Evangelist? Pastor-teacher? Where do you fit in?

ARE YOU AN APOSTLE?

Didn't Jesus have just 12 apostles? Yes. Then, how could a person today be an apostle? Easy! The word "apostle" means "one who is sent." Obviously there were many more people sent out on missions than just the Twelve special ones who walked with Jesus when He was here.

Look at 1 Corinthians 15:5-7, where Paul says that Christ appeared to the Twelve, and then "to the apostles." Here are the names of a few more apostles beside the Twelve: Paul (Gal. 1:1); Epaphroditus (Phil. 2:25, where the NASB translates "messenger"); Barnabas (Acts 4:36); Titus (2 Cor. 8:23, NASB "messenger"); Silvanus and Timothy (1 Thess. 1:1, cf. 2:6); Andronicus and Junias (Rom. 16:7); James, the Lord's brother (Gal. 1:19).

Some apostles were used in a special way to write books of the Bible. To them, God gave special and direct communication. Their teaching became the foundation of the church (Eph. 2:20). These men are called "holy apostles and prophets" (3:5). The word holy means "separated" or "set apart."

A certain group of apostles and prophets were set apart to write Scripture. Today there is no more need for that kind of apostle or for the Twelve who walked with Jesus. The names of the Twelve will be special forever (cf. Matt. 19:28 and Rev. 21:14). The Scriptures are completed.

The other apostles noted above—others who were "sent out" were not special friends who walked with Jesus, nor did they write any Scripture. What did they do? They were the missionaries of Bible times. They, like Paul, traveled from place to place planting churches and building up the new believers. They were responsible for leadership development in these new churches. That's why Paul told Timothy and Titus to ordain (or select) elders (bishops) in every church. That's the work of an apostle. (See Acts 14:21-28 for a complete breakdown on what these apostles or church-planters were doing.)

> *Apostles, church planters, pioneer missionaries—call them whatever you want, but we still need them!*

We still need apostles in this sense today. Maybe the word should be changed to identify with modern terminology, but they are still needed. With over 2 billion people in the world who have yet to hear the gospel of Christ, we still need the pioneer types. Do you have a desire to travel? Would you like the joy of building something from the bottom up? Do you like to start something, get it going, and then turn it over to others?

I had the joy of doing the work of an apostle or church-planter. It took me longer than the apostle Paul, but then that's understandable—I'm not the apostle Paul! I spent about three-and-a-half years establishing a church in Columbus, Ohio. It was loads of fun (as well as some heartaches)! God blessed, people were saved, leaders developed and the church grew. Its present leadership is doing so much better with that ministry than I ever did, but I was there when it all started. What a joy! What a privilege!

Apostles, church planters, pioneer missionaries—call them whatever you want, but we still need them! Are you interested? Has God placed that desire in your heart? Does it stay with you most of the time? What's holding you back?

ARE YOU A PROPHET?

If you ask the question, "Are you a prophet?" in some circles it is a joke. If you think of a prophet as a predictor of the future, then we certainly don't need them today. The Bible is sufficient to tell us about the future and how things are going to turn out. But the idea of a prophet as one who foretells the future is a product of the Middle Ages.

The word prophet means "to speak before." Not only can it refer to one who speaks about a thing before it happens, but in its common usage in Bible times it can refer to one who speaks before a crowd of people. In ancient society, a prophet was a public speaker. Prophets were what we call preachers. In the church at Antioch there were both prophets and teachers (see Acts 13:1). The prophets were proclaimers of God's truth.

God told prophets what to say. There was a sense of urgency and importance about their message. Aaron was a prophet, and under God's direction he was simply a mouthpiece for Moses (see Exod. 7:1). Some prophets in the New Testament predicted the future (Agabus—see Acts 11:28), while others simply relayed a message that brought encouragement and strength to believers (Judas and Silas—see Acts 15:32).

The purpose of prophesying was to speak to men for edification, exhortation and consolation (see 1 Cor. 14:3). The gift was also used to bring conviction to the nonbeliever (see 1 Cor. 14:24).

I overheard a lady say when referring to a recent guest speaker in our church, "He's a preacher, but not much of a teacher!" I have also heard that in reverse, "He's a teacher, but no preacher!" Perhaps we should look to the matter of gifts before we become too critical of the different kinds of spiritual leaders. If prophesying is related to *forthtelling* rather than *foretelling*, then it might parallel today's references to preaching, rather than predictors of the future.

If the prophet's ministry was to be a public speaker, to speak before the crowds, then we could easily visualize the need for prophets as well as pastor-teachers in the ministry of the local church. It might be possible to conclude that the larger a church grows (larger the crowd), the more necessary it is to have the "preacher-type" who can communicate effectively with the large crowd.

"Teacher-types" do well in smaller groups and classroom situations. Both preachers and teachers are needed. There is a sense in which a man who preaches should also teach, and one who teaches should also preach. One is concerned with content (teacher) and the other with application (preacher). One cares about what is communicated (teacher), and the other with how it is communicated (preacher).

It is my opinion (not dogmatic, just thinking about it!) that we have both types in the ministry of our church and among our pastoral staff. We have men of the Word who are excellent teachers (both young and old), but who have difficulty communicating before a large crowd of people. It affects their whole presentation.

We have others who love to "preach" to the large crowd, whether in the pulpit or at the beach, or in a college environment with hundreds of students. Some seem gifted as communicators and motivators, while others are outstanding in study, research and teaching content. There is room for both in the ministry of the church. It is time that we recognize gifts. There are enormous differences and people and ministries that need biblical explanation.

ARE YOU AN EVANGELIST?

Only one man is called an evangelist in the Bible—Philip (see Acts 21:8). He was one of the original seven chosen in Acts 6 to help the apostles in handling the distribution of food to needy widows. He was a godly man and faithful in ministry in the Jerusalem church. However, God led him into a ministry of evangelism in Samaria (see Acts 8) as well as in other places. He eventually settled down in Caesarea where he raised his family.

What did Philip do? He preached Christ. He told people about Jesus. He shared with many in Samaria as well as with one Ethiopian eunuch who was returning from Jerusalem in his chariot. An evangelist is a teller of the good news. His greatest joy is found in telling folks how to become a Christian and leading them to a knowledge of Christ. Philip also baptized those who responded to his message. After all, that is a vital part of the Great Commission of our Lord (see Matt. 28:19, 20).

We have men on our staff who I believe are evangelists. There are lots more among the members of our church. I have observed a few things about these particular men over the years. They do not enjoy sitting at a desk all day unless they are talking to someone about Christ. They are people-oriented. They love to be around people. They love to talk with people wherever they are. They are outgoing, and their zeal is contagious.

Typically, evangelists do not feel at home when studying or doing research. They must push themselves to study and teach. Everyone must study the Bible, but to them it does not come easily. They love the Word and use it constantly, but doing a word study for hours in an office is not their thing! If they go for weeks without seeing someone come to Christ they are depressed and burdened. Their greatest desire is to see people come to know Christ. They are great examples to all of us in how to share our faith. I have also observed that they lead more people to Christ than staff members with other gifts.

> *We should not try to make everyone feel as we do about ministering. Instead, we should recognize the differences and seek to build up one another.*

What about you? Are you an evangelist? Do you desire to talk with people about the Lord? Do you feel discouraged when you do not have that opportunity? Do you love people? Would you rather talk to a person than work at a desk? These questions and many more should be asked of every person who believes he is gifted in evangelism. All believers are responsible to witness, but not all are gifted by God. Those with the gift of evangelist can be of great help in training others how to share their faith in Christ.

It is also important to keep evangelists free to do their ministry. A layman in our church who seems gifted in evangelism was greatly discouraged one day. He was told by another Christian that if he did not disciple those he led to Christ, he was not obedient to Christ. He told me about his job and the time he had available. He shared with me that during the previous three months he had led eight people to Christ. He had no time to disciple them nor did he feel that desire.

I went to the person who told him to disciple his converts, and explained that those gifted in evangelism should be kept free to do that ministry and that others could help in the discipling of these converts—namely, him! He saw the point, and began immediately to help his brother to meet the needs of those new converts. We are all needed in the Body of Christ, but our gifts are different. We should not try to make everyone feel as we do about ministering. Instead, we should recognize the differences and seek to build up one another.

ARE YOU A PASTOR-TEACHER?

Are pastors the same as teachers, and is every pastor responsible to be a teacher? Could not some be teachers and not be pastors? Because gifts are different both in type and in the way they are used, we must be careful about being too dogmatic about the use of gifts. However, Ephesians 4:11 does make pastors the same as teachers. The Greek construction of that verse demands that there are four gifted leaders mentioned, not five. In that context at least, a pastor is the same as a teacher, and a teacher the same as a pastor.

A pastor is a shepherd, responsible to provide food and protection for his sheep. In order to provide food, he must be a teacher of God's Word. Not every pastor has the spiritual gift of teaching mentioned in Romans 12:7; but every pastor has the responsibility to teach. Not every elder in a church is a pastor-teacher (see 1 Tim. 5:17), but those who are pastors are to be teachers.

Several years ago a young man in our ministry felt that God was calling him to leadership as a pastor-teacher. I encouraged him to begin his ministry in the local church where he could be observed and his desires and gifts could be confirmed by others. Each class or Bible study he got involved with as a teacher declined in attendance. People were gracious, but frankly, he could not teach.

Finally, he came to me about this matter. We talked it over and discussed the importance of spiritual gifts. We noted that it is important to recognize what gifts we don't have so that we can begin to concentrate on gifts we do have. He got the point! He has a fine ministry now, but not as a pastor-teacher. I have often wondered what kind of frustration and discouragement would be in his life now if I had tried to persuade him to be a pastor-teacher in spite of what his ministry in that area had proven to be!

The wisdom of putting the two words pastor and teacher together to describe the ministry of this gifted leader is obvious. Some teachers have no desire to minister to people. They do not have a "shepherd's heart." Some who have the understanding and compassion of a pastor, do not desire to teach nor do any study of God's Word. Balance is so important.

A pastor-teacher's goals center on the maturity of believers. Some leaders reveal their lack of a pastor-teacher's heart by what concerns them. If the main focus of your ministry is planting churches, then maybe you're an apostle; if your primary concern is winning people to Christ, then maybe you're an evangelist; if your great love and desire is preaching and proclaiming God's Word to multitudes, then maybe you're the prophet; and if you love to work with a group of people you call your flock and watch them grow to maturity and begin to minister to one another, then maybe you're a pastor-teacher.

Leadership in God's church is based on ability. But it is ability that God gives. Gifts are the result of grace. We do nothing to deserve them or earn them. Christ gave these gifted leaders to the church, and He equips them with His authority and ability to minister to others.

It is important to discover if you are one of these four leaders. It will immediately tell you the kind of ministry you should develop. It will give direction to your life and relieve you of much frustration in trying to be something or someone you are not.

☑ LEADER'S CHECKLIST

1. Do you believe that God has chosen you as a leader for His church? Write down some reasons why you feel this way.
2. Do you have the desire of the apostle, to build churches and train leaders to take over when you leave?
3. Do you believe God has called you to preach?
4. Are you an effective public speaker? How can you tell?
5. Do you enjoy talking to people about Christ? How do they usually respond?
6. Would you rather share your faith in Christ with nonbelievers, than spend most of your time building up other believers?
7. Do you desire to minister to a group of believers you can call your own?
8. Do you tend to concentrate on the maturity of believers, rather than the salvation of nonbelievers?
9. Do you love to teach God's Word, and to study for that ministry?

8
DO SPIRITUAL GIFTS HELP?

AMONG the many spiritual gifts listed in the New Testament are two gifts that refer to leadership. One we shall call the gift of leadership itself (see Rom. 12:8), which is also translated "ruling," or "managing." The other we shall call the gift of administration (see 1 Cor. 12:28), which is also called "governments."

For many years now I have noticed enormous differences in the leadership styles of people in the ministry. I have tried to look for common ingredients that will help us build leaders for the future. Often I ran into a dead-end street! A few basic elements, however, kept coming to my attention. I wasn't always sure why these things existed, but they were there. Let me explain what I'm talking about!

- Some leaders were motivators; some were organizers.
- Some worked best in front of people; others at a desk.
- Some ad-libbed much of the time; others needed a chart or job description.

- Some demanded specific goals; others liked to solve present problems.
- Some cared little about costs; others always had dollar signs before them.
- Some derived authority from others; others had authority in themselves.
- Some organized around people; others organized around jobs and tasks.
- Some were excitable; others were stable and calm.
- Some were filled with new ideas; others spent time evaluating ideas.
- Some kept no schedules; others were very disciplined.
- Some had cluttered desks; others were spotless.
- Some were fun people to be around; others were dry, dull, and boring.
- Some loved to talk; others said very little.

The list could go on and on. There were tremendous differences in people. Yet, each was a leader. Styles were different, but all produced results.

What can we learn from all this? Differences do exist. Don't be too critical of another's leadership. Perhaps if we study the passages that describe the gift of leadership we will have a better understanding of the different styles of leadership.

DO YOU HAVE THE GIFT OF LEADERSHIP?

In Romans 12:8 Paul identifies a leader as "he who leads, with diligence." The word "leads" is based on two words, "to stand" and "before." To stand before people is the root idea of this gift of leadership. It refers to a person who motivates others and sees leadership primarily as it relates to people, not tasks. It is used eight times in the New

Testament, as well as several times in the Greek Old Testament.

In the New Testament, it refers to the father in a family (see 1 Tim. 3:4,12), to bishops (see 1 Tim. 3:5), deacons (see 1 Tim. 3:12), elders (see 1 Tim. 5:17) and believers who meet needs and do good works (see Titus 3:8,14). The

> *The Bible teaches that the one with the gift of helps is one who desires to help others by meeting their needs.*

word was used in Greek literature before Christ in the sense of presiding or conducting meetings. Another idea was that of protector. Out of this came meanings of assisting, helping and caring for others. Let's consider some of the facts about this gift.

It Appears in One's Home Life

This aspect of leadership is a qualification of elders (bishops) and deacons which is based on their home life (see 1 Tim. 3:4,5,12). It refers to the way a man handles his children. He leads them by keeping them under control with all dignity. Dignity points to a seriousness of purpose and self-respect.

One's children should reflect their understanding of the position of their father. The father should reflect a seriousness about his family, considering their needs of discipline, teaching and proper motivation. They should look up to his leadership.

A Sense of Urgency

We have noted that Paul connects this aspect of leadership with *diligence* (see Rom. 12:8). The description of this spiritual gift includes a simple phrase that is given in order to help us identify the kind of leadership that is given by the Holy Spirit. The words "with diligence" refer to "haste" or "speed." The one who has this gift is noted for the speed with which he responds to needs that exist. Those who take their time about responding are evidencing that the spiritual gift is not there, or that they are not being obedient to the promptings of the Spirit of God.

Wanting to Help

The gift of leadership flows from a desire to meet needs (see Titus 3:8,14). In contrast to those who see leadership as one who gives orders to other people, the Bible teaches that the one with this gift is one who desires to help others by meeting their needs.

In order to accomplish this (according to Titus 3:1), one must involve himself in what Titus calls "good deeds." This fits with our Lord's constant instruction that those who would be greatest and in positions of authority must learn to serve others.

It is interesting to see how important Paul believed good deeds are. In Titus 2:7, Paul says, "In all things show yourself to be an example of good deeds." Then in Titus 2:14, he says that one of the purposes of redemption is to have a people who are "zealous for good deeds." Titus 3:1 states that we are "to be ready for every good deed." And, of course, the admonition in Titus 3:8 and 14 connects "good deeds" with our word for "leadership," and emphasizes that these good deeds will meet pressing needs in the lives of those for whom the leader is responsible.

Taking Care of People

First Timothy 3:5 puts the word for leadership in parallel structure with the words "take care of." Leadership means taking care of people. The words "take care of" involve the direction of the mind toward the object cared for. It suggests loving interest and certainly the idea of protection.

> *The very sound of the word "administration" frightens many people.... But it has to be done!*

The story of the Good Samaritan in Luke 10 is a good illustration of this. In verses 34 and 35 the same word used in 1 Timothy 3:5 is used and translated to "take care of." When the Good Samaritan finished caring for the injured man's wounds, he brought him to the inn and, according to verse 35, he provided some money for the innkeeper and said, "Take care of him." He then promised to pay any additional expenses.

This illustration of taking care of people involves the matter of material or financial provision, and therefore includes physical needs. Those with the gift of spiritual leadership would obviously be caring for the spiritual needs of the people under their leadership.

A man's responsibility to take care of his family involves providing for their needs, protecting them from danger along the way, and maintaining discipline and control as the leader of the home. A spiritual leader must also take care of those for whom he is responsible. There must be a proper sense of authority and chain of command, but it appears that the response factor to his leadership is based upon the qualities of his home life as well as his loving concern for those around him.

A good leader is a protector of people, and understands that "love covers a multitude of sins." He cares for the personal needs of those he leads, seeking their good at all times. He is known by his "good deeds" in seeking to meet the needs in people's lives.

While all those in positions of leadership should seek to emulate these principles, some are uniquely gifted by God. Such leaders lead not by training, education or natural talent, but because of God's grace and the unique ministry of the Holy Spirit. What a joy it is to work with those in whom we see the Spirit-controlled life and temperament, as well as with those who are gifted by the Holy Spirit for that ministry of leadership.

Motivational Gifts

The person with the gift of leadership will usually be a motivator of others. He works out of a desire to see people grow and develop. He will lead in order to meet needs. When a need exists, he responds quickly. He loves to set goals for other people and to work by them himself. He has a sense of accomplishment when goals are completed. He organizes primarily through people. He spends most of his time in leadership talking with people, helping them to see their problems and how they can be more effective.

One of our staff members who fits this picture came to my office to discuss his ministry. Our entire conversation dealt with the goals he had for himself and others. It was amusing as well as thrilling. God made him like that, and he is doing a tremendous job. He sees his worth and value through the goals he has set. As long as his goals are based on biblical and spiritual objectives, God will bless his leadership.

DO YOU HAVE THE GIFT OF ADMINISTRATION?

The very sound of the word "administration" frightens many people! Administration is the dirty word that is necessary in every organization. It is a thankless job that rarely is appreciated by others. But it has to be done!

Those who do administration without a gift in that area can be quickly spotted. They are frustrated with details and complain about having too much to do. They procrastinate. Things pile up on them. There never seems to be enough time to get things done. They are uptight with people. They worry. They're overwhelmed with the responsibility they have. They need a break (so does everyone else!).

The word "administration" in 1 Corinthians 12:28 is used three times in the New Testament and several times in the Greek Old Testament. It means to "steer a ship." It refers to the pilot or helmsman. The word "guide" was often used to describe the work of this person in ancient times.

The same word is used in Proverbs 12:5 in the Greek Old Testament, in reference to the wicked: "The thoughts of the righteous are just, but the *counsels* of the wicked are deceitful." Throughout Proverbs the word carries the idea of counsel, especially as it relates to guidance or direction.

Outside the Bible, the word is used in the writings of Plato to refer to one who knows the times of the day and the year, the sky, the stars, currents of air, etc. This knowledge was, of course, beneficial to keeping a ship on course. Our modern idea of "navigator" would fit this usage. We can learn several things about the gift of administration from the way the word is used in these sources.

Setting the Course

Those with the gift of administration are responsible for setting our course or direction. Although a ship's helmsman was not the owner of the ship in ancient times, he was responsible for steering it. He may also not be the ship's captain (see Acts 27:11). Sometimes we confuse the responsibility and accountability of one who owns the ship with the one who has been employed to run the affairs of the ship in terms of getting it to its proper destination.

If the ship is to be taken as the local church (as was frequently the case in the early church), then the owner would be the Lord, and the helmsman could refer to those responsible for the direction of the church. The helmsman must navigate the ship on a proper course. He keeps the ship from losing its way and from running into various dangers along the way.

A person who has this gift makes decisions that affect the direction in which the "ship" (or church) should go. Obviously, this should be the direction in which the Word of God teaches it should go! The person with this gift is therefore concerned about keeping the church (or any group within it) on course with what the Word of God says it should be doing.

Making Decisions

We have all heard the phrase, "the buck stops here." The point is that the chain of command must stop at some person's desk, and a final decision made. When the safety of the cargo and passengers is at stake, one must be able to make decisions that will guarantee the safe arrival of the ship at its proper destination.

The ability to make decisions is an important function of the gift of administration. Sometimes this means cutting back on methods, practices, personnel, financial support, etc., in order to keep the "ship" on a safe course! While every one of us must make decisions from time to time, not all of us have that God-given ability to make decisions in behalf of many others. There is much risk involved, and the danger of failure is constantly in front of you. But,

---

Those with the gift of administration sense accountability for what happens, while those with the gift of leadership make things happen.

---

those with the gift have the God-given courage and ability to make those decisions.

The goal for believers is maturity (see Col. 1:28). Those with the gift of administration would therefore also be concerned about any methods or practices that would detract from that goal. They would concentrate on that which moves people toward maturity.

The Helmsman's Character
Proverbs 12:5 points out that the counsels (words) of the wicked are deceitful. (See the lamentation of the helmsmen or pilots of the ships of Tarshish in Ezekiel 27:25ff.) In contrast, straightforward counsel and a godly life-style are required to make the decisions of the "helmsman" what they should be. Sinful practices will diminish our ability to make correct decisions in terms of spiritual leadership.

A Sense of Responsibility
Those with the gift of administration have a strong sense of responsibility and accountability. We can certainly see

that in terms of a ship's cargo and passengers. How tragic it would be to have a person making decisions that affect the lives of many people without any sense of responsibility toward those people! But the real issue here in terms of accountability is that the "helmsman" does not own the ship, but is employed by and fully accountable to the owner for the safe arrival of the cargo and passengers.

In spiritual matters, the owner is the Lord Himself. This point is clearly emphasized in Hebrews 13:17 when it says: "Obey your leaders, and submit to them; for they keep watch over your souls, as *those who will give an account*. Let them do this with joy and not with grief, for this would be unprofitable for you" (italics added). The One to whom we must give account is the Lord Himself. Romans 14:12 says, "So then each one of us shall give account of himself to God." Leaders are answerable to God for the decisions they make and the direction they give.

In Stormy Seas

At no time is the gift of administration more sorely needed than in stormy times. When things are running smoothly no one seems to notice the presence of the "helmsman," nor do they sense their need of his direction and leadership. But when the waves of life come pouring over the sides of our ship, and the storm increases in intensity, then everyone must out of necessity look to the "helmsman" for leadership. The test of one with the gift of administration is the ability to "weather the storm" and to steer the ship back on course.

There are many "storms" along the way in the work of God. Churches and Christian organizations often seem to be sinking, or at least they seem to be tossed around by the waves of difficulty and trials. At a time like that, spiritual leaders with the gift of administration are greatly needed.

They bring calm into the hearts of those in the storm, and decisions are made which will bring the "ship" safely through the storm.

Those with the gift of administration sense accountability for what happens, while those with the gift of leadership make things happen. The administrator can put it on paper much easier than can the one with the gift of leadership.

Some leadership types would rather talk with people. The administrator needs time alone away from people. He must think carefully about the decisions that are to be made. The one with the gift of leadership responds immediately to a need, while the administrator needs time to think about its ramifications and effects on others. The leadership person wonders why we can't do it now; the administrator knows why.

These two gifts make a great team! Two are better than one, provided that they understand each other's gifts and allow each other the freedom to exercise those gifts. What is missing in the administrator is found in the gift of leadership, and vice versa. They need each other.

It was my joy to experience the struggles of leadership and administration with a dear friend in the ministry. He and I worked together for seven years. He now has a great and growing ministry of his own. We learned much about each other and the differences between us. Time and maturity have shown us many similarities. We are both leaders. We both love to teach and preach.

He is a better motivator than I, and I learned so many things from him. I think in some ways, I am a better administrator, and I hope he learned from me. We are still good friends (in case you wondered!). We both struggled with the study of spiritual gifts, and saw how very important it was to our relationship with each other.

Some are gifted and some are not. Often we must do what we do even though we are not gifted in that area. We exercise a role in that situation. There is a sense in which all of us can exercise leadership, trusting God to help us. If we have the spiritual gifts for leadership, our task is easier. Regardless, we can all learn the principles of these gifts and profit by them, with God's strength.

☑Leader's Checklist

1. Do you like to work with people more than with specific tasks? What are some clues that tell you which you prefer?
2. Do you desire to meet needs immediately when you see them?
3. Do you sense a desire to take care of people under your leadership?
4. Do you feel responsible for things? How many things? Do you have to "do it all"?
5. Can you make decisions quickly in times of stress and difficulty?
6. Are you willing to take risks in order to grow as a person? Can you name three recent instances in which you took risks?

9

CAN WOMEN BE USED IN LEADERSHIP?

IT almost seems to be wasted effort even to ask the question. The reading material and video programming in today's society is filled with scores of incidents and illustrations that prove and demonstrate a woman's role in leadership. No discrimination is allowed, yet women still lag behind in salaries and key leadership positions.

More women today are seen in politics and executive positions in major corporations than ever before. The pressure is on men to accept the role of women in leadership and to acknowledge their right to assume any role which men have traditionally been holding.

CONTINUING CONCERNS

But all is not well in the movement to demand for women full equality with male counterparts. Some things seem to call for different treatment, such as pregnancy and bodily function, and many women are demanding more understanding and support in such concerns.

The growth in the numbers of women returning to the role and responsibility of homemaker has clearly brought confusion to many women who have argued and pushed for equality in the marketplace. Women in the work force have necessitated the spread and growth of child care centers, and the accompanying problems in the development of such children are only now beginning to be noticed and evaluated.

Divorce is higher in homes where both husband and wife are working and at the same time trying to raise children. Single parents are growing in number and the majority by far are women who are divorced and have entered the work force but still must maintain some degree of family life for their children. Some have described these facts as a "disaster" and a "tragedy" for the American family.

THE CHURCH CONNECTION

In the churches of our culture, there is a growing awareness of women in leadership roles. The ordination of women continues as a controversial and divisive matter in many denominations. Hundreds of churches, especially in rural areas, are now pastored by women.

Women have been placed on pastoral staffs in increasing numbers over the past 20 years. These women serve in leadership capacities that vary from children's ministries to presidents of Christian colleges and universities. Many women have joined the pastoral teams of large churches in the capacity of Director of Women's Ministries.

Thousands of churches still question the placement of women on church boards, believing that this is a violation of biblical teaching, while thousands of other churches have been including women on their boards for several years now. The problem does not seem to go away.

In some areas, the battle is over, and women are accepted on an equal basis with men in all areas of church life and leadership.

However, the truth is that thousands of Christians are still wrestling with this problem and are not sure of the biblical teaching on the issue. Nor are they convinced as to the practical consequences such decisions will bring to church life and practice.

WHAT IS THE BASIC PROBLEM?

The problem for Christians deals with our understanding and interpretation of key biblical passages that deal with the relationship between men and women. Galatians 3:28 makes a clear statement about equality in terms of our relationship to Jesus Christ: "There is neither Jew nor Greek, there is neither slave nor free man, there is neither male nor female; for you are all one in Christ Jesus." Class and gender distinctions are removed in the body of Jesus Christ, where we all become brothers and sisters in the Lord and equal at the foot of the cross.

The major passages that cause confusion and controversy are found in 1 Corinthians 11:1-16, 14:26-39 and 1 Timothy 2:8-15. In addition to these passages, there are several related issues in Romans 16:1-2, Ephesians 5:22-33, Colossians 3:18-25, 1 Timothy 3:1-13, Titus 1:5-9, and 1 Peter 3:1-7.

The problems dealing with women in leadership in the church fall into the following categories:

1. A wife's submission to her husband.

2. A restriction on preaching and teaching.
3. A requirement to be silent in public services.
4. The qualifications for elder/bishop and deacon.

Are Women to Be Submissive to Men?

Many societies in the Middle East and in third world countries would immediately answer yes to the question. Many church leaders in the past and present have also felt that the Bible teaches this.

To Husbands or Men in General?

First Corinthians 11:3 is often cited as evidence that women should be submissive to men in general: "But I want you to understand that Christ is the head of every man, and the man is the head of a woman, and God is the head of Christ."

This entire passage (1 Cor. 11:1-16) deals with the unique relationship of men and women in public worship. Women are exhorted to cover their heads, and men are told not to do so. One of the issues in this passage deals with the length of hair, and Bible students and scholars alike argue over whether a literal covering (hat or bonnet) is required, or whether the simple fact that a woman's hair is a covering will suffice.

Verses 14,15 say clearly: "Does not even nature itself teach you that if a man has long hair, it is a dishonor to him, but if a woman has long hair, it is a glory to her? For her hair is given to her for a covering."

The whole discussion is built on the teaching of verse 3 regarding the statement, "the man is the head of a woman." Is Paul arguing that all women are under the authority and leadership of all men?

Ephesians 5:22-24 teaches: "Wives, be subject to your

own husbands, as to the Lord. For the husband is the head of the wife, as Christ also is the head of the church, He Himself being the Savior of the body. But as the church is subject to Christ, so also the wives ought to be to their husbands in everything."

The phrase "the head of the wife" is the same as in 1

> *The Bible teaches the submission of a wife to her own husband, not to anyone else's husband or to any other man.*

Corinthians 11:3, except here the English translation makes it clear that the word for "woman" refers to a man's wife. The Greek word *(gunaikes)* can refer to a woman in general, single or married, or to a wife. The context must determine the correct translation in English.

The Bible is consistent in its teaching, and not contradictory in its statements. The phrase in 1 Corinthians 11:3 is referring to the leadership of the husband over his own wife, not all men over all women! The Bible teaches the submission of a wife to her *own* husband, not to anyone else's husband or to any other man.

In Public Worship
The same problem exists in 1 Corinthians 14:26-39, which deals with the use of prophecy and speaking in tongues in public worship services of the church. In verses 34-36 we read the following:

Let the women keep silent in the churches; for

> they are not permitted to speak, but let them sub-
> ject themselves, just as the Law also says. And if
> they desire to learn anything, let them ask their
> own husbands at home; for it is improper for a
> woman to speak in church. Was it from you that
> the word of God first went forth? Or has it come to
> you only?

Once again, the context makes it clear that the word
"women" is referring to "wives," not women in general.
This exhortation deals with the submission of a wife to
her husband's leadership and exhorts her not to speak out
in a public meeting, thus undermining his role and responsibility as a leader in his home. The proper thing is to ask
him at home in private.

The same problem is found in 1 Timothy 2:8-12:

> Therefore I want the men in every place to pray,
> lifting up holy hands, without wrath and dissen-
> sion. Likewise, I want women to adorn themselves
> with proper clothing, modestly and discreetly, not
> with braided hair and gold or pearls or costly gar-
> ments; but rather by means of good works, as befits
> women making a claim to godliness. Let a woman
> quietly receive instruction with entire submissive-
> ness. But I do not allow a woman to teach or exer-
> cise authority over a man, but to remain quiet.

When the Bible says "let a woman quietly receive
instruction with entire submissiveness" it is referring to a
wife's submission to her husband. When the text says "I do
not allow a woman to teach or exercise authority over a
man" it should read "wife" and "husband."

The Greek language uses two primary words for "man."

One (*anthropos*) refers to man in general. Another word (*aner*) is more specific, and is necessary in the context if the interpretation refers to a "husband." In all three cases, 1 Corinthians 11:3, 14:34-36, and 1 Timothy 2:11-12, the Greek word for "man" is a derivative of *aner*, not *anthropos*.

God is concerned about the relationship of a wife to her husband, and that message is clear. Wives are to submit to their own husbands, not any other man. That submission is not talking about the general responsibilities of submitting to authority which are common to both men and women; it is dealing with a wife's special and unique relationship to her husband. She is not to give that unique submission to any other man, only her husband.

The church does not overrule, disregard, or change the relationship of a wife to her husband. Some cults and male-dominated churches have tried to persuade wives to be submissive to the church leadership as they would to their own husbands. The result is always disastrous and disruptive to marriage and the families involved.

CAN WOMEN TEACH AND PREACH?

The first thing we need to deal with is the perceived difference between the "pulpit" in a church sanctuary or auditorium, and the "lecture stand" in the Sunday School classroom. Some churches allow women to teach in the classrooms of the church, but believe it to be wrong for a woman to stand behind the pulpit of the church. That sort of thinking gets in the way. Pulpits and lecture stands are simple amoral items, things to be used and regarded as we see fit. Nothing in the Bible makes such a distinction.

As we have noted, 1 Corinthians 11:1-16 speaks of women who "prophesy" in the public meetings of the church. Some believe that this refers to receiving special and direct revelation from God on the spur of the moment, and that it needs to be shared immediately. Others take the word "prophesy" to mean public preaching.

The preposition "before," contained in the Greek word, can mean "before something happens," or "in front of (before) a group or audience." The latter viewpoint is the most commonly used interpretation for the setting in biblical times. Whether the public speaking involves future events or simply proclaims what God has already said, whether it is past history or predicted future events, does not affect our point here. The fact is, women were involved in proclaiming God's Word in the public assembly of the church.

Some women in the Bible are called "prophets." Luke 2:36 refers to a prophetess named Anna. Deborah, who judged Israel as their political leader, is called a prophetess in Judges 4:4. Philip the evangelist had four daughters who were prophetesses (Acts 21:9). The simple fact: women were involved in the public proclamation of God's Word.

The problem comes when we evaluate the words of 1 Timothy 2:12: "But I do not allow a woman to teach or exercise authority over a man, but to remain quiet."

As indicated earlier, the word "woman" should be "wife" and the word "man" should be translated "husband." The meaning of the verbal infinitive "to teach" is clarified by the parallel phrase "exercise authority." The issue here is the relationship of a husband and a wife. A wife is never to undermine her husband's authority over her. His authority serves as a protective umbrella that God honors in her life.

With permission and encouragement of her husband, there is no reason why a wife could not exercise her gifts of teaching or preaching, but it will always present some danger to the Bible's teaching about marriage. Teaching God's Word does become a matter of authority.

This wonderful Book reveals what God has said. It is in this Book that we read, over and over, "Thus says the Lord" and "the word of the Lord came unto me." These statements ring with authority from God Himself.

In a marriage seminar I conducted years ago, I inter-

> *"God has gifted my wife with great teaching and leadership ability. I am 100 percent behind her, and by the way...I gave her permission!"*

viewed a woman with outstanding gifts of leadership, administration and teaching ability. Since the subject of that particular session in the seminar was on the submission of the wife to her husband, the audience found her example particularly intriguing. The question was posed to her, "How can you exercise such leadership in the church and at the same time be submissive to your husband?"

At that point, I interrupted before she could answer. Knowing that her husband was sitting in the front row, I said to the audience, "Why don't we ask her husband how he handles this problem?" I know her husband well. He doesn't like to talk very much. He is the strong, silent type. He loves to work with his hands and is a real man's man, a former athlete, tall, big and very strong. I will not easily forget his response that day. He reluctantly came up to the microphone, quietly told me that I "owed him one for this," and proceeded to answer the question with the following statement:

"God has gifted my wife with great teaching and leadership ability. I am 100 percent behind her, and by the way...I gave her permission!" The audience broke out in spontaneous applause. It was one of those rare moments to treasure long in the memory.

Wives need the support, encouragement and permission of their husbands. When that is missing, there are usually problems that occur within that woman's ministry. When the husband is supportive, the questions go away, and the woman exercises her leadership with effectiveness. Men respond to a woman's leadership when they know that her husband is supportive of her and that there are no problems in their relationship with one another in marriage.

CAN WOMEN BE ORDAINED AS PASTORS?

In some denominations, pastors are considered to be elders. In that case, the Bible's teaching would not allow a woman to serve as pastor. Elders/bishops are to be husbands and fathers. However, if a given local church had elders who were husbands and fathers, and did not automatically consider their pastors to be elders, then it would technically be possible for a woman to be used as a pastor and not violate the biblical teaching regarding elders/bishops. The elders of the church could use the ministry of a woman as pastor and still maintain the overall authority for the decisions and policies of that church.

It is not an easy matter to settle, and it has become a very serious controversy among Christians. I remember the difficulty some 20 years ago of having a woman on the pastoral staff of the church. Our church took a bold step and placed a woman in a key staff position. She did not serve as one of the elders, but they employed her services and encouraged her ministry. It proved to be a tremendous blessing to all of us.

Since that time, it has been my privilege to work with several women in the leadership of the pastoral staffs where I have served. These women have proven by their life and godly example that women can be used in the leadership of local churches when they do not serve as elders, but operate under the authority of the elders.

I have seen great examples of leadership, administration and teaching ability among godly women. Efforts geared to keeping women out of leadership are counterproductive and hurtful to the ministry of the church. Using women in leadership need not violate the teaching of the Bible.

As long as most churches regard their preaching and teaching pastors as elders, it will be very difficult for women to be ordained and serve in those roles. The position of authority which a teaching and preaching ministry gives to a person presents a unique problem for wives who must not usurp the authority of their husbands. It is a difficult problem, but not insurmountable. Godly women will manifest the delicate balance between a commitment to use their gifts for the Lord and a desire to obey the Scripture's admonitions about a wife's relationship to her husband.

WHAT IS A GODLY WOMAN?

Titus 2:3-5 gives us the instruction we need for women who desire to serve as leaders in God's church.

> Older women likewise are to be reverent in their behavior, not malicious gossips, nor enslaved to much wine, teaching what is good, that they may

> encourage the young women to love their hus-
> bands, to love their children, to be sensible, pure,
> workers at home, kind, being subject to their own
> husbands, that the word of God may not be dis-
> honored.

The word "likewise" puts this teaching about godly
women in direct comparison with the instruction for older
men (Titus 2:2) and younger men (2:6-8). It is a part of
that which is described as "sound (healthy) doctrine."
Sound doctrine is healthy teaching that affects the life-
style of the people who believe it. Three things are said
here about godly women:

**1. A godly woman is concerned about her relationship
to the Lord.** She is described as one who is "reverent in
behavior." The word "reverent" refers to something sacred,
as well as fitting or proper. Her behavior is fitting to God
and His standards.

She has convictions that are based on the Word of God,
not her own opinions. In all she teaches, the content centers in what is intrinsically good or virtuous. The phrase in
Titus 2:3, "teaching what is good," is a statement referring
to ethics and morality.

Verse 5 states that her testimony and reputation is
important to her. She does not want the word of God to be
dishonored ("blasphemed," *KJV*). Her life is a constant witness of one who walks with the Lord and is concerned
about her life and behavior patterns in the eyes of others.

**2. A godly woman is controlled in her responses
toward others.** Titus 2:3-5 describes her control in several
areas:

    a. Verbal control—"not malicious gossips."
    b. Social control—"nor enslaved to much wine."

c. Emotional control—"sensible."
d. Sexual control—"pure."
e. Self control—"kind (does that which is useful or beneficial to others)."

Godly women control themselves. First Timothy 3:11 says of women in leadership that they must be "dignified, not malicious gossips, but temperate, faithful in all things." First Timothy 2:9-10 adds: "Likewise, I want women to adorn themselves with proper clothing, modestly and discreetly, not with braided hair and gold or pearls or costly garments; but rather by means of good works, as befits women making a claim to godliness."

"Proper" clothing refers to that which is well-arranged or neat. When a woman dresses "modestly and discreetly" she is concerned not only for her own desires but also is careful about soliciting other men sexually. She does not allow her inner beauty to be smothered by outward display. God is not against jewelry, hairstyling or beautiful clothes; He warns here about extravagance, about confidence in the external to the ignoring of the internal. First Peter 3:3-4 puts it this way:

> And let not your adornment be merely external—braiding the hair, and wearing gold jewelry, or putting on dresses; but let it be the hidden person of the heart, with the imperishable quality of a gentle and quiet spirit, which is precious in the sight of God.

Godly women dress to please the Lord as well as their husbands. They do not seek to entice or allure men other than their own husbands by what they wear. Our world simply is not careful in these matters. But Christians walk to a different tune than the one the secular world is playing. We must constantly evaluate all that the world promotes and encourages us to buy and wear, especially in the area of clothing. In choosing our clothing we must ask, Is it pleasing to the Lord? Does it encourage sexual enticement and cause others to believe that we are seeking to be immoral and "loose"?

3. A godly woman is committed to her responsibilities at home. When my wife and I were applying for a mortgage on our home, the loan officer asked her, "And, what do you do, Mrs. Hocking?" She said, "I'm a homemaker." The officer replied, "But, do you have a regular job?" She answered, "It *is* a regular job, and the best job in the whole world!" After that response, the loan officer decided to move on in our deliberations!

A godly woman is a lover of her husband and her children (Titus 2:4). The Greek word here is from *philia*, which refers to the kind of love that includes close friendship. A godly woman is a friend to her husband and her children. Her high regard for her home is reflected in the phrase "workers at home."

The woman of Proverbs 31:10-31 was quite industrious and handled many business and financial transactions; but her home was her primary responsibility and privilege. The godly woman has a sincere respect for her husband's role and leadership. As the text says, she is "subject" to her own husband so that God's Word would not be "blasphemed."

Godly women are needed in the leadership of our churches—women who do not violate the biblical standards of submission to their husbands, nor desire to usurp their husbands' authority. Godly women do not seek to be elders of the church or to be in positions of authority to prove their equality with men. They are servants of the

Lord who use their gifts of leadership, administration and teaching to be examples to others and pleasing to the Lord. We need them, and may God increase their number in our local churches!

☑ Leader's Checklist

1. Are women to be submissive to men?
2. Why do you think most churches are reluctant to use women in key leadership positions?
3. What examples would you give of how women in the Bible were used in leadership roles?
4. Why can't women be elders or bishops in the church?
5. Do you believe that it is possible for women to be pastors in local churches? Why?
6. What is the problem with ordaining women?
7. What is a godly woman?
8. Can you give an example of a woman in leadership today who seems to fulfill the biblical responsibilities and maintains a godly submission to her husband? What qualities do you see in her that others could emulate?

LAW IV

MOTIVATION:

YOU NEED TO KNOW WHY YOU WANT TO BE A LEADER

10

BE CAREFUL ABOUT YOURSELF

WHY do we do what we do? Jeremiah 17:9,10 seems to indicate that we cannot know ourselves; that we are deceitful and wicked. Only God knows what we are really like. That's why we need to study His manual (Bible). In it God reveals much about our motivations.

THE IMPORTANCE OF MOTIVATION

The business world is concerned about motivation because corporate profits are involved. Views today of success and failure are often related to motivation. The so-called "goodies" of life (Christians call these "blessings") are seemingly reserved for those who are highly motivated.

The advertising industry is concerned with motivation. Ads tell us frequently why what we are wearing is no good anymore. They remind us that the "things" we have are getting old and in sad need of repair. We are being motivated to buy a new product, of course.

Psychologists have long been aware of the importance

of motivation. Behavior patterns, whether good or bad, can be directly traced to the motivations people have. Decisions, major or minor, are affected by motivations. Much time is spent in introspection and analysis of why people react the way we do.

Motivation is a vital topic in leadership, too. People quickly question the wisdom of a leader's decision today because they have been affected by leaders with wrong motives yesterday. We hear such things as "He's in it for himself," or "I'm going to get what's coming to me," or "They're all alike; you can't trust them!" When someone appears to be successful, people will say, "If you really knew him, you would know why he's doing that!" We question people's motives.

There are six areas in which the spiritual leader must be especially careful about his motivation. In each area there is an improper motivation that can destroy the effectiveness of the spiritual leader.

Be Careful About a Position Which Leads to Pride

The desire of one who wants to be first in everything is rooted in pride, which the Lord hates (see Prov. 6:17).

Pride vs. Service
Pride is concerned about lofty titles and fancy offices. It covets public recognition and seeks to parade itself before the eyes of others. A person motivated by position is inclined more to emphasize his authority than his service to others.

Position blinds your eyes to the feelings of those around or under you. Decisions are made without understanding and compassion. Authority is viewed as a title or job description (which, of course, is a part of it), rather than a responsibility that only God can help you fulfill.

In saying all of this, we do not mean that titles, offices and job descriptions are unimportant or should be disregarded. God has a chain of command in the home, church, government, business, etc. We are instructed to be

---

The best leader has a servant's heart. He shows no partiality, but learns to be "slave to all."

---

submissive to all kinds of authority, regardless of the motivations or spiritual caliber of those in authority. It is the attitude of the leader that is our concern, not the responsibility of those under that leadership.

Jesus illustrated this problem in His remarks about the scribes and Pharisees (see Matt. 23:6-12). Their problem was the desire for honor and position. They loved the "place of honor" and the "chief seats in the synagogues." They wanted to be treated with respect. They knew little of what it is to be a servant.

Three basic motivations explain a leader's desire for position.

The Desire for Ultimate Authority. It's hard for people motivated by position to be subservient to others. On every decision and plan they desire to be the final answer. There is a time when those in authority must make the final decision, but any leader with experience and much responsibility will quickly tell you what a burden such authority can be upon your life.

Your decisions affect the lives of other people. The best leader has a servant's heart. He shows no partiality, but learns to be "slave of all" (see Mark 10:42-45).

The Desire to Dominate. The desire to control and dominate others can arise out of a poor and insecure self-image. If a person is insecure in himself or in his job he will tend to dominate others. It gives him a measure of satisfaction to know that he can control others.

The feeling arises out of pride, not humility. It fails to recognize the importance of each individual. It refuses to accept differences of opinion. Sometimes a leader's fear of failure results in a desire to dominate. He tries to hide his own mistakes and inadequacies before others by dominating and controlling.

The Desire to Be Admired. Some people want to be leaders simply because they think high position makes people take notice. The leader motivated by position feels that the "best seats" and the "better service" goes to the people of great position. The desire to have others respect you is a reflection on your self-esteem.

Respect is the result of a godly life-style and consistent character, not high position. If your life-style is not pleasing to the Lord, people can outwardly appear respectful, but inwardly resent your leadership.

I once knew a man who was controlled by the desire for high position. It was manifested in the way he talked, walked and dressed. People who worked for him said he was proud and domineering. A visit to his office revealed his problem. All kinds of awards, plaques, trophies and letters of commendation cluttered his office. They seemed to be "security blankets." I felt sorry for the man. He was lonely, unhappy and very insecure.

What's the solution to this problem of leadership to which we all are tempted? *Humility*; evaluating yourself in the light of God's approval and commendation; being a servant to all. That's the only solution. Away with all the props that are artificial and superficial, the little crutches we lean on to prove how important we are. Be done with lesser things. *Graduate* to the role of servant. That's the place of greatest joy!

BE CAREFUL ABOUT MONEY AS YOUR MOTIVATION

Motivations in the secular world are often controlled by the dollar sign. As we have seen (chapter 6), Christian leaders also need to be very careful about themselves in the area of money. Money is not sinful in itself, but loving it is (see 1 Tim. 6:10). You are not spiritual because you are poor. But money is simply a tool, not a master to control you (see Matt. 6:24). Money-love or the desire to get rich can cause many other problems (see 1 Tim. 6:9,10).

A friend of mine left the ministry because of bad debts. He was not careful and it cost him his leadership. Another friend left the ministry because money became more important to him than ministry. He enjoyed being rich and the pleasures money could afford. He also lost his leadership.

Why does money cause such problems? Why do leaders forfeit the blessing of God upon their ministry for a few shekels? How does money affect the exercise of spiritual leadership? Ask yourself three questions.

Am I a Leader Because I Am Paid?

When your reason for doing what you do is because you are paid for it or because it is a requirement that affects your salary, then your leadership is weakened. Some pastors evaluate the Lord's will in leading them to a church on the basis of the salary they will be paid. It is best to make such a decision without knowing what the salary will be. If it is more than you make now, you might want the job for the wrong reason; if it is less than you make now, you might reject it for the wrong reason.

Several years ago I was traveling to a meeting without a great deal of money in my pocket. In fact, I wasn't sure I could return without getting some gas for my car. On the way there I began thinking about the honorarium I might receive, even though none was promised. I thought about how much it should be, and what my reactions would be upon receiving it. I wondered if I should ask for it in cash so I could get the gas I needed to get home.

I decided to keep quiet about an honorarium; but I stood around after the meeting waiting for some assurance about it. None was given. As I got in my car to drive home, I found a root of bitterness growing. I soon realized that my motive was completely wrong in speaking at that occasion. I was doing it because of the possibility of being paid. Well, the Lord didn't let me off the hook on that one! I never did get an honorarium! (By the way, the gas miraculously lasted until I got home!)

Churches and Christian organizations should take care of the financial arrangements of guests who minister to them as surely as the leaders who are daily ministering to them. Leaders should not be muzzled or hindered in their work by the lack of financial support. But on the other hand, leaders should not do what they do because of the money they might receive. We must do it as unto the Lord. He alone must control our motivations.

Do I Lead Because I Need the Money?
Some people don't get motivated at all unless they need

the money. It seems more and more difficult to get people to respond without paying them. In many cases, we ought to pay people for what they do. On the other hand, there are many situations in which pay is not justified. It can rob the individual of serving voluntarily. If you do something because you need the money and it is not the payment you expected or wanted, you will soon discover a spirit of resentment or personal hurt.

Do I Lead Because I Want to Get Rich?

Many leaders today are doing what they are doing because of a desire for financial gain. Money is the number one motivation. Paul warned us about this problem in 1 Timothy 6:9,10. It is hard to respect a person as a spiritual leader, much less respond to them, when you know that wealth is the motivation.

What's the answer to the problem of money? How does a leader avoid the wrong motivations? One word answers—*contentment*. Paul wrote of this quality in Philippians 4:11-13, and spoke of what he had learned. God has promised to supply our needs. We need to trust Him. In 1 Timothy 6:7, Paul tells us that we brought nothing into this world and we will take nothing out of it. Godliness with contentment is great gain. Contentment is based on inward trust in a faithful God who has promised to supply all your need (see Phil. 4:19).

BE CAREFUL ABOUT WANTING TO BE FAMOUS

Fame is in the heart of the leader who is impressed by his own achievements. The leader troubled by this problem loves to read his "press clippings." He's concerned with proper introductions and resumes with long lists of honors. He evaluates his effectiveness by who knows about him.

One day certain Jewish leaders sent priests and Levites from Jerusalem to meet John the Baptist in the wilderness. They wanted to know who he thought he was. John told them, "I am a voice of one crying in the wilderness" (John 1:23). He said his ministry was to prepare the way of the Lord. He didn't feel worthy to untie the thong of the Lord's

Leadership is lonely, and sometimes the need for encouragement is so great that a person exercises leadership only to have the encouragement of others. Watch out!

sandal. Referring to Jesus, he remarked in John 3:30: "He must increase, but I must decrease."

Paul wrote in Galatians 6:14, "But may it never be that I should boast, except in the cross of our Lord Jesus Christ, through which the world has been crucified to me, and I to the world."

Some want fame because they desire people to know how great they are. Others want it because they want to be like someone else. Some feel it makes them important. Proverbs 27:2 says, "Let another praise you, and not your own mouth; a stranger, and not your own lips." Our one desire should be the glory of God Himself. In 1 Corinthians 1:29 Paul says that "no man should boast before God," and in verse 31 of the same chapter, "Let him who boasts, boast in the Lord."

A person whose life is controlled by wanting to be

famous needs *self-denial*. By self-denial we don't mean asceticism or false humility, but the desire to give all the glory to God. It is a willingness to be unnoticed so that Jesus is recognized by all. It is putting aside selfish ambition, submitting yourself to the Lord of all, who alone is worthy of praise! Practicing self-denial is a commitment to praise and thank God for everything. To Him be all the glory!

BE CAREFUL ABOUT PERSONAL NEEDS

The fourth motivational problem facing the leader is in the area of personal needs. Leaders should be primarily motivated by the needs of others. Everyone has the following needs. The danger is when leadership is exercised solely in order to fulfill them.

We Need Encouragement

Everyone needs the encouragement of others. But leadership is lonely, and sometimes the need for encouragement is so great that a person exercises leadership only to have the encouragement of others. Watch out! The Lord knows your needs before you ask Him. We are to bear the burdens of others (see Gal. 6:2), and learn to bear our own (see Gal. 6:5).

Self-pity can set in on the leader who becomes overwhelmed by the loneliness of leadership. The result can be laziness, apathy and indifference. Sometimes we need a "kick in the pants," rather than the sympathy of others!

The only solution is to *trust God to meet your needs*. The Lord is "the God of all comfort," and He understands better than anyone else. Take your burdens to the Lord and leave them there! Cast all your anxiety upon Him, He cares for you (see 1 Pet. 5:7).

We Need Physical Affection

Everybody likes "strokes"—not only emotional support but physical expressions of affection. A warm handshake, an arm around the shoulder, a brief embrace, a pat on the back are simple but effective ways to say, "I love you" or "I appreciate you."

But, it's dangerous to exercise leadership out of a need for physical affection. Leaders seem especially vulnerable in this area. It's almost a paradox: strong leaders seem above such a need, yet all leaders know how lonely they can become and how welcome is a show of affection.

Ecclesiastes 3 reminds us that there is a time for everything. Often the problem in showing physical affection is one of timing. A few suggestions for leaders:

1. Don't give physical affection out of a sexual need, except to your marital partner. When you feel aroused in a situation or attracted by the opposite sex, it is dangerous to show physical affection.

A friend of mine was in his office, counseling with a lady who was quite attractive. She was having marriage problems and was near an emotional breakdown. With many tears she embraced my friend for a moment of comfort. In that moment, they both felt a strong attraction toward one another. One thing led to another, and after several weeks of continual counseling and contact, they went too far. Both lives were damaged.

When evaluating the situation much later after repentance and restoration, my friend realized that at the time he had a sexual need. He and his wife were not ministering to one another as the Bible teaches. His desires got the best of him.

2. Don't give physical affection to members of the opposite sex when you are alone or isolated from other people. This is only common sense, but the testimony of

many leaders supports the wisdom of repeating it. Jesus told us that "The spirit is willing, but the flesh is weak" (Matt. 26:41). Don't trust your ability to control your desires! Trust God, and do all you can to prevent trouble before it happens.

The answer to the problem of personal needs in the heart of the leader is *trust in the Lord*. There is no substitution! "The Lord is my shepherd, I shall not want" (Ps. 23:1). He has promised to meet our needs. Trust Him to do it!

Be Careful About Feeling Obligated

Duty can be a good thing, but it can also lead to improper motivations. Some leaders feel obligated to lead; they are unhappy and weary with the responsibility of leadership; there is a lack of joy and enthusiasm.

Such a leader does what he does because he thinks if he didn't, people would not like him as much. He feels an obligation to perform in order to have people respond to him. On the other side of the coin, the leader sometimes feels that if he doesn't do what is expected of him, people will consider him to be a failure. The fear of failure drives many a leader!

Another problem is that of guilt. Some leaders feel guilty if they do not do what is expected of them. Therefore, they work harder out of obligation than before. Guilt drives them.

The obligation many feel in being a leader arises out of a bad self-image or a lack of self-worth. Often, this leader has not learned to accept himself in the light of God's love and forgiveness. The leader fails to rest in the Lord. He is pressuring himself to perform.

The only answer to this motivational problem is *the joy of the Holy Spirit*. Lead because you are thrilled with the opportunity! Joy goes out the window when we do not relax in the love of God and enjoy the people around us. There is little joy when we impose standards upon ourselves that no one else put there. God loves you, leader! He can fill your heart with joy in exercising your leadership. You have value because of God—it's as simple as that!

BEWARE THE "SUCCESS SYNDROME"

Some leaders lead entirely in order to meet their goals. Aims and objectives are the chief motivating force in their lives. Goals are good, but they become improper when controlled by the "more" syndrome. We want to achieve "more than last year." Such a leader must do better than the previous year or he senses failure.

The desire to achieve can be good and productive, but it can also detract and hinder us in accomplishing the will of God. Some leaders are pressured by "success-oriented" people. They have charts and diagrams to prove their point (and often their value). Behind this is the matter of comparison. Some leaders spend all their free moments comparing themselves with other leaders, trying to prove to themselves that they are doing better or more than others. Numbers play an important part to leaders motivated by achievement. Numbers become the test of "success." If more people were involved this week over last, this month over last, or this year over last, then they are successful.

What's the answer to this problem? *Peace*, resting in the sovereignty of God. Evaluating yourself with others is not the answer. Neither are apathy and indifference. Resting in the Lord is the answer. His "well done" is given on the basis of faithfulness. He judges us for what we have done for Him, not in comparison to another's gifts, talents or achievements.

SUMMARY

In summary, let us review the problems leaders may encounter, and the solutions the Bible offers.

Position

The problem of position, which can lead to pride, is solved by *humility*. Jesus' answer to the person who wants position is illustrated in Mark 10. James and John said to Him, "Grant that we may sit in Your glory, one on Your right, and one on Your left" (v. 37). Jesus answers:

> "To sit on My right or on My left, this is not Mine to give; but it is for those for whom it has been prepared." And hearing this, the ten began to feel indignant toward James and John. And calling them to Himself, Jesus said to them, "You know that those who are recognized as rulers of the Gentiles lord it over them; and their great men exercise authority over them. But it is not so among you, but whoever wishes to become great among you shall be your servant; and whoever wishes to be first among you shall be slave of all. For even the Son of Man did not come to be served, but to serve, and to give His life a ransom for many" (vv. 40-45).

The Love of Money

To the problem of the love of money, Paul said that the solution was *contentment*:

> Not that I speak from want; for I have learned to be content in whatever circumstances I am. I know how to get along with humble means, and I also

know how to live in prosperity; in any and every circumstance I have learned the secret of being filled and going hungry, both of having abundance and suffering need. I can do all things through Him who strengthens me....And my God shall supply all your needs according to His riches in glory in Christ Jesus (Phil. 4:11-13,19).

Fame

The solution to the problem of wanting fame is to learn *self-denial*. We noted Paul's statement in 1 Corinthians 1:29,31: "No man should boast before God...Let him who boasts, boast in the Lord." John the Baptist said of Christ, "He must increase, but I must decrease" (John 3:30).

Personal Need

The concern for *personal needs* can be solved by *trusting* in God. Peter says to cast "all your anxiety upon Him, because He cares for you" (1 Pet. 5:7). David says "the Lord is my shepherd, I shall not want" (Psalm 23:1).

Obligation

The leader who leads because he feels obligated to serve lacks *joy* and enthusiasm. Paul says in Romans 14:17, "For the kingdom of God is...righteousness and peace and joy in the Holy Spirit."

Achievement Goals

Finally, the leader who finds his motivation in achieving, is evaluating himself with others. He needs to rest in the Lord, to find *peace*. "Thou wilt keep him in perfect peace, whose mind is stayed on thee: because he trusteth in thee" (Isa. 26:3, *KJV*).

☑LEADER'S CHECKLIST

1. Have you ever sought a higher position in order to feel important? Describe the situation.
2. On a scale of 1-10, rate yourself on why you work as a leader.

   1   2   3   4   5   6   7   8   9   10
   For what I receive   For what I give

3. Do you want to get rich?
4. Do you refrain from drawing praise from others, but rather redirect it toward the Lord?
5. Do you have personal needs that you are failing to trust God for? List these.
6. Do you sense that you do what you do out of obligation rather than joy? What can you do about this?
7. Do you spend a good deal of time comparing yourself with others? To whom do you compare yourself? Why?
8. Do you do what you do because you feel guilty if you don't? Name some instances.
9. Do numbers affect your leadership? Do you get discouraged easily when the numbers are less? Do large numbers make you proud?

11
Doing Things for the Right Reasons

WHY are some leaders driven by wrong motives such as those discussed in the previous chapter? Sin, of course, will do it every time! But, what other matters make a leader susceptible to inadequate motivations? How can a leader be sure he is doing things for the right reasons?

In the early years of my ministry as a leader I did not understand these things as clearly as I see them now. It seems to take experience itself to show you how these things can affect your leadership. I have always wanted to do God's will and to live for His glory, but sometimes I get in the way. I don't mean to, it just comes naturally!

The following seven problems have greatly affected my leadership at one time or another. Excuse me for being so personal, but I don't know any other way to share with you what I believe is important for all leaders to understand.

What Factors Lead to Wrong Motivations?

When Results Are Not Visible

Leaders often doubt and question their leadership when they do not achieve visible results immediately. But before you get completely depressed and write that letter of resignation (usually on Monday mornings!), you'd better keep a few things in mind.

First of all, you may have the wrong set of results in your mind and heart. You may be set more on numbers and charts than on individual people who are being built up and encouraged by your leadership. God told Isaiah to go and tell people His message, *even though He also said they would not respond* (see Isa. 6). Most of us would have quit right there and then! Isaiah's responsibility was to be faithful to God, regardless of the results.

Secondly, the problem may be a lack of faith and vision on your part, and that is why you see so few results. Don't blame the people. *You* are the leader! What do you believe God can do in your situation? Without faith, you can't please the Lord (see Heb. 11:6). God honors our faith. He is sovereign in what He does, but I have discovered that He coincides His sovereignty with my faith in Him so that my joy is made full!

Thirdly, you may not be working hard enough. Some of us don't seem to enjoy work. Maybe you are lazy and indifferent, and that is why you see such few results. You need to get right with God and get to work! God puts no premium on laziness or apathy.

A staff member in our church was ready to give up due to a lack of results in his ministry. I tried to sympathize and encourage him, but it didn't seem to help. Then, one of the secretaries told me how lazy he was and that the work was piling up. He was not following through on contacts that were given him, nor answering his telephone calls. He spent many hours at his desk just thinking (a necessary thing at times, but it can be overdone).

After putting the facts together, I called him into my office, and this time the conversation was not one of sympathy and encouragement—it was get to work or get another job! It was amazing to me how quickly his attitude changed, as well as the results in his ministry.

Inability to Handle Criticism

Some leaders don't handle criticism from others very well. Some get mad, and some cry. Some get ulcers, and some seek revenge by using their leadership to hurt or hinder those criticizing.

The only way I know to avoid criticism is to say nothing, do nothing and be nothing (printed on a plaque in my office). But saying that still doesn't mean I like to be criticized. Who does? My problem is the same as yours—learning how to handle criticism when it comes, and in my case, it's a weekly problem.

First, realize the possibility that you may deserve it. I know this hurts to admit, but sometimes leaders deserve the criticism they are receiving. Maybe what people are saying is the truth! Can you face it? Can you learn from it?

Second, you may create that kind of environment. If you are a critical person, you can expect to receive much of it in return. The older I get the more aware I am of the damaging effects of criticism that is not biblical and constructive. I don't want to listen to it, yet there's something about my old sin nature that wants to be critical of others and to hear criticism about other people. Lord, deliver us!

I try to avoid hearing what critical people have to say. I don't want to be around them. If I can't say something nice about a person, why say anything at all? I realize that at times criticism may be justified and right, but much of what I have seen that people call "constructive criticism" is questionable. Be careful what you say concerning others. Learn to compliment them and look for the positive qualities in their lives.

When someone shares a critical remark about another person with you, learn to answer with a positive statement concerning that person. Find something commendable in that person's life and draw attention to it. Your leadership will grow.

Third, remember that criticism is intended to make us stronger as leaders, not weaker. When criticism comes your way and you know it is not justified, learn to accept it and be thankful for it anyway, knowing that God will use the experience to make you stronger. It will help you to reflect more of His love toward others. Many times we learn what not to do by the things people say about us. That's worth something, you know!

No leader can expect to be free from criticism. The very fact that you are a leader opens the door for others to criticize you. You are out front, easy to spot and easy to blame. When someone makes a critical remark to you, just say "Thank you." Sometimes you can say, "Thanks for telling me about that; I'm sure the Lord had a reason behind the fact that you told me." Another positive way to respond is, "Thank you for caring enough about me to criticize me." Or, you can say, "Please pray for me that I will learn to do things as God wants me to do."

Lack of Cooperation

This can eat your heart out if you don't watch it! You begin to question your leadership because others are not cooperating. But before your motivations get all confused, ask yourself two questions. The first one is, "Do the people know what to do?" If they don't, how can you expect them to cooperate? It's really not their fault. A lack of communication or information on what to do can produce this condition.

One fall we planned to have a tremendous outreach program. But we started too late and failed to communi-

> *There are different levels and kinds of friendship. You do not have to receive everything you need from one person.*

cate properly to the people. It was no surprise that very few people showed up for this great adventure!

The second question is, "Are you leading the way in this matter?" If you are asking people to do something that you will not do, then it is no surprise that there is little cooperation.

Another important thing to rely upon when there is little cooperation is the fact that you and God make a majority! Leaders need to stand alone at times. Some people are waiting to cooperate in order to first see the kind of courage you have as a leader.

Loneliness as a Leader

Very few people (leaders are an exception) will understand what it's like to be a leader. They will not know what you are going through, and they will not know how to help. That friend you need is hard to find. Of course, the Lord is with you, so you are never really alone (see Matt. 28:20;

Heb. 13:5). Here are a few suggestions that I have found helpful in meeting the problem of loneliness.

Be aware of what different friends have to offer. There are different levels and kinds of friendship. You do not have to receive everything you need from one person. Some people will be social friends that are fun to have dinner with or with whom you can enjoy a bit of recreation.

Other friends are great for just talking by the fireplace or over a cup of coffee. You need people who can listen well without being critical. Some friends are great in a crisis, they seem like family. You can call on them for an emergency. There are a few in leadership positions who do understand, and under proper conditions you will find close friendships with them.

One caution about close friendships with other leaders: Make sure there is no competition between you, and that you do not constantly compare yourself with the other leader or his ministry.

The major hurdle to get over is trying to do everything with one person or another couple. It usually doesn't work that way. Learn to enjoy friendships with many people and don't have too many expectations about what you will receive from them. If you enjoy a friendship with someone by participating in athletic competition, don't assume that your marital partners will be good friends also. My wife may enjoy shopping with a particular lady, but it doesn't mean that that lady's husband and I will be close friends.

Remember that intimate friendships take time. It has been my observation that close friendships take a long time to develop. Be patient and don't try to be close right away. There is a time for building confidence between you and your friend. Most friendships we have are really acquaintances or based on social occasions. The circle of friends in this category can be great. Enjoy them all!

There are closer friendships in life that are built on serious communication or a time of deep need or crisis. There is something "special" about those friends that were there to help when you needed it. The circle of friends like this is much smaller.

Intimate friends with whom you can share anything without fear of being rejected or criticized compose a very small circle. Some people have only one other intimate friend besides their marital partner in their entire life. Most of us probably would not have more than five to 10 intimate friends in our lifetimes.

When I sense deep loneliness, for whatever reason, I must remember first that the Lord is with me and to share my feelings with Him. Secondly, I turn to those intimate friends with whom I can freely talk. My wife is my best friend in that regard! In addition to my wife, I have found my best friends to be those with whom I have worked in our church.

Seek out friends. Before you let self-pity and discouragement grip you in a time of loneliness, ask yourself if *you* are seeking to be a friend to anyone. It is more important to *be* a friend than to *have* one. In fact, when you seek to be a friend to others it seems that God rewards you with friends who will minister to you.

Having said all of this, I must still remind every leader and leader-to-be that loneliness is a price to pay in being a spiritual leader. The higher you are in the levels of any organization, the more loneliness you will sense. Learn to accept it and to trust God to meet your need.

An Excessive Work Load

Sometimes our work load just seems too great to bear. The danger here is that you start doing things to solve this problem that are unwise or based on hasty decisions. The next day or the next week may be a different situation. You may feel differently about a heavy work load after a few days pass.

But what if you don't? Suppose you are continually swamped, and there is no letting up. What do you do?

First, you should consider some of the reasons why you are experiencing the heavy work load. Here are some possibilities.

1. You are incompetent (ouch!) to meet the demands of the job.
2. No one is competent to meet the demands of the job! (That's better!).
3. No staff or lay job descriptions: There is constant overlap and neglect so that the job usually falls back on your desk.
4. You can't trust others to do what you are doing.
5. You take on too much work that no one told you to do (you're probably a "workaholic").
6. Your priorities are all messed up.
7. You are physically tired or emotionally exhausted.
8. You like people to think you are busy and overworked.
9. You're nervous and keyed up most of the time—you *must* work.
10. You think the organization depends so much upon you that if you don't keep at it, everything will fall apart!

Enough of the problems! What about some solutions? Here are two practical suggestions.

1. Make a list. The first thing some leaders do each morning is to make a list of things they want to accomplish that day, and they check them off when completed.

Others make their "things to do" list the night before so they can sleep better! Don't procrastinate! If you can do it today, then do it. Don't put something off until tomorrow that you could really do today. Strive for a clean desk every day.

2. Ask whether you need an assistant. You may really need someone to help alleviate your heavy work load. It might be a secretary or another leader who can take over some of your responsibilities. Determine what things you presently do that could be done by others. Evaluate those things that are better done by you as well as that which must be done by you. Some of the "better" category needs to be entrusted to others.

A good executive secretary may be a better choice than another leader like you. A good secretary is better for tasks that are routine. Interruptions can be controlled, and many things presently done by the leader can be performed by a good secretary. A secretary might be able to meet the needs of several leaders, and thus not only help you, but others.

But be careful about hiring an assistant. That suggests that you cannot do your job and need help. It also makes you the "growth-restricting" obstacle. The assistant is limited by your direction and approval. It is better to view your helper as an "associate" than an "assistant." You are partners even though you may have the final decision on major matters.

It is better to delegate areas of ministry to another leader if you are trying to manage too many ministry areas yourself. Maybe the new leader you hire will do things differently than you, and even do them better. Give him total responsibility in a given area of ministry and let him run with it. Let him rise and fall by himself. He will grow faster and appreciate you more.

Disharmony and Disunity

A lack of harmony and unity is a heavy burden for any leader to bear. Loyalty and love are the two most important ingredients among people who work together. Disunity can greatly affect the leader's motivations. In a desire to solve the problem, leaders can act too hastily or without proper information and facts.

A co-worker spoke to me one day about what he thought was disloyalty on the part of another worker. The worker was doing something that I do not do, and did appear to be disloyal. The person who shared this with me did not realize that I had told the worker in question what I would do, but that he could do whatever he wanted. I trusted him completely. He was not disloyal; he was simply doing his job another way—and it proved to be more effective than the way I usually handle that situation.

When real disunity and disloyalty (not hearsay or someone's opinions) occur, how should you handle the problem? These things have helped me in those difficult situations and times of tension and stress.

1. Identify the problem. Make sure you have the facts clearly.
2. Learn to face it and deal with it. It just doesn't go away by itself.
3. Recognize the real source of the problem (see Jas. 3:14-16; 4:1).
4. Express love to all concerned and seek their best interest.
5. Be willing to listen to all sides and viewpoints.
6. Emphasize prayer, confidence in God and getting things right with Him first.
7. Be tolerant and forgiving, seek to restore rather than sever relationships.

8. Thank God for the problem. He has allowed it, so learn from it.
9. Determine whether the situation demands the removal of a staff member. If the disloyalty continues after confrontation, then the removal must happen or other serious problems will develop.

Every situation is, of course, different. Leaders need the wisdom of God. If I can put my finger on the problem that

Don't seek sympathy from others all the time. If you can't handle the problems, how can others who follow your leadership expect to handle theirs?

most often occurs, it is the failure of leaders to deal quickly with situations that arise. We hope they will go away. My experience tells me differently. Deal with them in love as soon as possible.

The Weight of Personal Problems
Leaders are not exempt from personal problems. Things like bad health, financial difficulty, marital disharmony and bad relationships in the family or with other people can all affect your motivation and your peace of mind. The pressure of these things can become so great that it starts affecting your leadership, and becomes noticeable to those who work with you. How do you handle this?

Begin by thanking God for the problems you're having (see Phil. 4:6,7), and seeking His wisdom and help through prayer and study of the Word. Don't seek sympathy from others all the time. If you can't handle the problems, how can others who follow your leadership expect to handle theirs?

Also, don't publicly refer to your personal problems. If people ask you in loving concern, then you might want to respond. But, don't parade your personal troubles before others. It will hinder their reaction to you as a leader. It will keep them from wanting your help in time of need.

Learn the principle that your personal problems are intended by God to help you share with others with compassion and empathy. Problems are designed to help you learn the secret of God's strength (see 2 Cor. 12:7-10). If you don't have problems, you're not human.

Hebrews 5:1,2 speaks about priests being chosen from among men so that they can deal gently with the ignorant and misguided, since they also are beset with weaknesses. People will not come to you for help if you are not human. They must understand that you know by experience what they are experiencing. This identification with people is vital to the role of spiritual leadership.

What Motives Should Spiritual Leaders Have?

We need to do things for the right reasons, and to have proper and biblical motives. The problems will be there and we have to face them. We cannot run away from problems. It's a part of what leadership is all about. But, we need to do things from proper motives. God will bless that. Our leadership will grow when the heart is right.

Make God's Glory Your First Priority

It all starts with the glory of God. First Corinthians 10:31

says to do everything to the glory of God. Whatever you do as a leader, ask yourself this one question, "Will this glorify God?" To glorify God is to honor and praise Him. It means to give Him all the credit.

Seek to Win the Lost

Whatever his primary responsibility, the spiritual leader must constantly seek to win the lost to Christ. He is to be all things to all men that we might by some means save a few (see 1 Cor. 9:19-22). He knows that the Great Commission is his job. He does not justify his obedience to Christ on the basis of his work with the saved. His work must also include the desire to win as many people to Christ as he possibly can.

Good leaders will seek to maintain balance in their leadership between the ministry with the believer and their evangelism of the nonbeliever. Frequently, leaders need to ask of what they do, "What is contributing to the salvation of lost people?" Determine what ministries are designed for the purpose of evangelism. If none exists, then the spiritual leadership in that organization is deficient.

Most evangelistic efforts in Christian organizations are designed to invite nonbelievers to attend meetings where believers are accustomed to go. If you want to penetrate your community for Christ, design efforts that are attractive to nonbelievers. Try a "Self-protection Clinic" for the women of the community, with Christian police officers conducting it and sharing the gospel during it.

Put on a men's breakfast (without charge) in a non-church environment (like a local restaurant), with a sports personality who loves Christ and knows how to communicate with nonbelievers. Have your young people provide a free car wash to the people of the community with appropriate gospel literature and witness. Establish some special seminars in marriage and family subjects that will appeal to nonbelievers and be especially designed to reach them.

Above all, learn to go where the people are, instead of expecting them to come to you. Reach out to them where they live. Speak their language. Provide services for them, such as counseling or day care centers. Constantly evaluate what you do as to how many contacts you are making with nonbelievers. The more contacts, the better the opportunities to win people to Christ.

It is wise to provide a program of training for believers on how to share their faith. This program should be carried on as a regular part of your ministry, thus emphasizing to everyone the priority of evangelism in the motives behind your leadership.

Seek the Maturity of Believers

Paul said he worked hard at the task of bringing believers to maturity (see Col. 1:28,29). Spiritual leaders are to equip the believers for ministry (see Eph. 4:11,12). Sometimes we use people to build our work rather than using our work to build people. The difference is enormous in terms of motivation! Keep emphasizing maturity and spiritual growth. Make sure what you do contributes to it. Seek to build up rather than tear down.

One day in a staff meeting we were evaluating a certain project. It seemed like a good idea and everyone was leaning toward it until one of the brothers asked what it would do to encourage the spiritual growth of our people. Silence. It was obviously not a project for evangelism, and it did not seem too valuable in developing maturity among our people. Then, why were we doing it? So much for a good idea! We went on to something else.

One more word about maturity. Make sure that the

growth you are talking about is spiritual. We are to grow in the grace and knowledge of Jesus Christ (see 2 Pet. 3:18).

Serve out of the Love of Christ

There are two ways to look at this motive. One is our love for Christ and what He's done for us. The other is His love for us, displayed through what He did at the Cross. Second Corinthians 5:14 seems to take the latter view. Christ died for us, thus demonstrating His love for us. That love He had for us at the Cross motivates or constrains us. He stimulates us to proper action by His love for us. That is the way it should be. We work better under conditions where love prevails.

When His love is compelling and controlling us, we will also love others (see 1 John 4:7ff). Most employees in Christian organizations expect the level of love to be greater than secular employment. That's only natural. A great deal of disappointment hits the Christian worker when the atmosphere resembles what he knew in the world. It need not be that way. Christians indwelt by the Holy Spirit have the capacity to love each other with God's love. Love is a tremendous motivating factor. More about this in a later chapter.

A Heavenly Reward

Some feel that a reward in heaven is not a worthy motivation for service. But the apostle Paul taught in 1 Corinthians 9:24-27 that the thought of an imperishable crown in the future was a motivating factor to the way he conducted his life. Jesus reminded us to lay up treasures in heaven and not on earth (see Matt. 6:19-21). Second Corinthians 5:10 states that we must all appear before the judgment seat of Christ. What believer has not been motivated by the thought of hearing Jesus say, "Well done, good and faithful servant; enter into the joy of the Lord" (see Matt. 25:21).

We have seen that it is important for the spiritual leader to do things for the right reasons. It affects the response of people as well as their respect. Certain problems can beset the leader, causing him at times to slip back to an unworthy motive. We all fail at times. It's a reminder to all spiritual leaders of their need to depend upon the Lord. May God help all of us to do things His way!

☑ Leader's Checklist

1. Have you considered why you have such few results? List some possible reasons.
2. Can you handle criticism from others without being discouraged? Think of some recent instances when you have been criticized. How did you handle it?
3. Do you know why people do not cooperate? List some possible reasons.
4. What do you do to meet the need of loneliness in your life?
5. Do you understand the importance of friends? How many close friends do you have? Name them. Do they know they are your close friends?
6. Why do you take on heavy work loads?
7. Would a secretary be a better assistant to you than another leader like yourself?
8. What steps would you take to deal with disunity and disloyalty?
9. Do you constantly refer to personal problems in your life? To whom?
10. Which of your motives are biblical and spiritual?

12
THE ULTIMATE PRIORITY

A S we have seen, motivation is serious business for leaders. We understand the need for our motives to be godly in every way.

THE HIGHEST MOTIVATION

First Corinthians 10:31 tells us to "do all to the glory of God." The ultimate priority for every leader is to glorify God in all we think, say and do.

Psalm 29:1-2 says: "Ascribe to the Lord, O sons of the mighty, ascribe to the Lord glory and strength. Ascribe to the Lord the glory due to His name; worship the Lord in holy array." Psalm 96:7-9 repeats that admonition, and Psalm 115:1 adds: "Not to us, O Lord, not to us, but to Thy name give glory because of Thy lovingkindness, because of Thy truth."

Glory belongs to the Lord. God's character deserves it. His creation also demands that we give Him glory, as the Bible makes clear in Revelation 4:9-11:

> And when the living creatures give glory and
> honor and thanks to Him who sits on the throne,
> to Him who lives forever and ever, the twenty-four
> elders will fall down before Him who sits on the
> throne, and will worship Him who lives forever
> and ever, and will cast their crowns before the
> throne, saying, "Worthy art Thou, our Lord and
> our God, to receive glory and honor and power;
> for Thou didst create all things, and because of Thy
> will they existed, and were created."

Psalm 19:1 says, "The heavens are telling of the glory of God; and their expanse is declaring the work of His hands." When men refuse to glorify God as they examine the wonders of His creation, they are "without excuse" before a holy God (Rom. 1:20-23). The "invisible" things of God are clearly seen by what He has made.

We observe in creation His glory, power and eternal nature. If we do not honor and glorify Him and give Him thanks, but rather turn the glory of the incorruptible God into some invention of our own hands, we deserve His wrath and judgment. We are without excuse!

HOW WE CAN GLORIFY GOD

But how do we, in fact, give glory to God? If that is the ultimate priority of spiritual leaders, how is it done?

God Is Glorified by Our Salvation

Without doing anything but believing the gospel, we bring glory to God! Why? For one thing, it exalts the grace of God that has made it all possible. Paul reveals this remarkable fact about our salvation:

Just as He chose us in Him before the foundation of the world, that we should be holy and blameless before Him. In love He predestined us to adoption as sons through Jesus Christ to Himself, according to the kind intention of His will, to the praise of the glory of His grace, which He freely bestowed on us in the Beloved (Eph. 1:4-6).

God's grace is glorified when we are saved because He saves us on the basis of His own sovereign choice, not our

---

God wants to use us more than we want to be used.

---

personal worthiness or human performance. Ephesians 2:8-9 reveals that we are saved by grace, not by our own works.

Our salvation also glorifies God because we are saved by His power, not our own ability. Paul writes that "we have this treasure in earthen vessels, that the surpassing greatness of the power may be of God and not from ourselves" (2 Cor. 4:7).

The "treasure" is the "light of the knowledge of the glory of God in the face of Christ" (v. 6). It is contained in clay pots, not worth much in themselves, but valuable because of the treasure within. Behind all of this, the text says, is the power of God. God is glorified and honored because it is His power alone that saves us, not our own ability. We cannot earn or deserve God's salvation.

God is also glorified in our salvation because it exalts His Son, our Lord and Savior, Jesus Christ. Philippians 2:9-11 makes this quite clear:

> Therefore also God highly exalted Him, and bestowed on Him the name which is above every name, that at the name of Jesus every knee should bow, of those who are in heaven, and on earth, and under the earth, and that every tongue should confess that Jesus Christ is Lord, to the glory of God the Father.

God is glorified when "every knee" bows, and "every tongue" confesses. When Jesus Christ is so recognized as King of kings and Lord of lords, God the Father is honored and glorified. Jesus said, "I glorified Thee on the earth, having accomplished the work which Thou hast given Me to do" (John 17:4). Jesus glorified His Father, and His Father is glorified when Jesus is exalted.

We Glorify God by Moral Purity
First Corinthians 6:18-20 is powerful:

> Flee immorality. Every other sin that a man commits is outside the body, but the immoral man sins against his own body. Or do you not know that your body is a temple of the Holy Spirit who is in you, whom you have from God, and that you are not your own? For you have been bought with a price: therefore glorify God in your body.

When leaders stay away from sexual sin, they are glorifying God in their bodies. Our bodies are instruments to be used for good, not evil. Paul gave Timothy this important instruction:

> Nevertheless, the firm foundation of God stands, having this seal, "The Lord knows those who are

His," and, "Let everyone who names the name of the Lord abstain from wickedness." Now in a large house there are not only gold and silver vessels, but also vessels of wood and of earthenware, and some to honor and some to dishonor. Therefore, if a man cleanses himself from these things, he will be a vessel for honor, sanctified, useful to the Master, prepared for every good work. Now flee from youthful lusts, and pursue righteousness, faith, love and peace, with those who call on the Lord from a pure heart (2 Tim. 2:19-22).

The usefulness and productivity of a spiritual leader's life is connected with moral purity. God wants to use us more than we want to be used. Our willingness to be used must be combined with a commitment to stay away from sexual sin. If we do not, then God will restrict our usefulness.

We Glorify God by Praise and Prayer

Jesus said in John 14:13, "Whatever you ask in My name, that will I do, that the Father may be glorified in the Son." In John 15:7-8, Jesus taught us: "If you abide in Me, and My words abide in you, ask whatever you wish, and it shall be done for you. By this is My Father glorified, that you bear much fruit, and so prove to be My disciples."

Psalm 50:23 says, "He who offers a sacrifice of thanksgiving honors Me." Jesus told us the importance of giving God glory and praise in Luke 17:11-19, the story of His healing of ten lepers. Although all were healed, only one returned to give glory and thanks to God. He was a Samaritan. Jesus said, "Were there not ten cleansed? But the nine—where are they? Was no one found who turned back to give glory to God, except this foreigner?" (vv. 17, 18).

God is glorified when we praise and thank Him for who He is and for all that He has done. Praise should be on the lips of all believers, but how much more on the lips of our spiritual leaders!

If the ultimate priority is to give glory to God, how can that be achieved in a leader's life if little time is given to prayer and praise? May God help us to understand what glorifies Him.

God Is Glorified by Good Works

Jesus said:

> You are the salt of the earth; but if the salt has become tasteless, how will it be made salty again? It is good for nothing anymore, except to be thrown out and trampled under foot by men. You are the light of the world. A city set on a hill cannot be hidden. Nor do men light a lamp, and put it under the peck-measure, but on the lampstand; and it gives light to all who are in the house. Let your light shine before men in such a way that they may see your good works, and glorify your Father who is in heaven (Matt. 5:13-16).

Our good works glorify our Father in heaven. We are "salt" and "light" to this world. Our lives were meant to be seen by others—this is the purpose of God. God is glorified when we shine for Him!

We Glorify God When We Suffer for Him

First Peter 4:12-16 reveals how we can glorify God in the present difficulties we may suffer.

> Beloved, do not be surprised at the fiery ordeal

among you, which comes upon you for your testing, as though some strange thing were happening to you; but to the degree that you share the sufferings of Christ, keep on rejoicing; so that also at the revelation of His glory, you may rejoice with exultation. If you are reviled for the name of Christ, you are blessed, because the Spirit of glory and of God rests upon you. By no means let any of you suffer as a murderer, or thief, or evildoer, or a troublesome meddler; but if anyone suffers as a Christian, let him not feel ashamed, but in that name let him glorify God.

Of course those who have died for the cause of Christ glorified God. When Jesus predicted Peter's death, John wrote, "Now this He said, signifying by what kind of death he would glorify God" (John 21:19).

In life and death, therefore, God is glorified. When we suffer for His sake—not because of our own mistakes and blunders—we bring God glory. We may not understand the "why" of our suffering, but one reason which should keep our hearts steady and our minds clear is that God wants to be glorified in all that we think, say and do. When we suffer unjustly and for our faith in the Lord Jesus Christ, God is glorified.

Using Spiritual Gifts in Ministry
First Peter 4:10-11 emphasizes the use and ministry of spiritual gifts and reminds us that this, too, brings glory to God:

As each one has received a special gift, employ it in serving one another, as good stewards of the manifold grace of God. Whoever speaks, let him speak, as it were, the utterances of God; whoever serves, let him do so as by the strength which God supplies; so that in all things God may be glorified through Jesus Christ, to whom belongs the glory and dominion forever and ever. Amen.

Whether a speaking or serving gift, God is glorified when we use it for Him. When we speak, we are to make sure that it is God's Word that we are proclaiming, not our own thoughts and ideas. God is glorified by His own Word. When we serve, we are to do it with the strength of the Lord. God is glorified when that occurs.

Paul wrote of how our ministry to one another, working with each other in the Body of Christ, can bring glory to God:

Now may the God who gives perseverance and encouragement grant you to be of the same mind with one another according to Christ Jesus; that with one accord you may with one voice glorify the God and Father of our Lord Jesus Christ (Rom. 15:5-6).

Our unity as believers gives glory to God as we seek to minister to each other, using our gifts and abilities to build up others and thus glorify our wonderful Lord!

☑ LEADER'S CHECKLIST

1. What is our ultimate priority?
2. Why should we glorify God?
3. How does our salvation glorify God?
4. Why does moral purity glorify God?
5. Are prayer and praise a part of your daily agenda? If

not, what could you do to strengthen your commitment to these things?

6. What difficulties have you experienced in which you have seen how God was glorified? Explain what happened.

7. How do spiritual gifts glorify God?

LAW V

AUTHORITY
People Need to Respond to Your Leadership

13

WHY DO PEOPLE RESIST AUTHORITY?

I T'S natural to resist authority! But knowing that doesn't always provide spiritual leaders with practical answers to practical problems. Interpersonal relationships in any Christian organization are affected greatly by the concepts of authority which are held by those people.

A pastor friend told me of his desire to "straighten out" a church that had a history of short pastorates. The problem, he said, was a lack of authority. People did not respond to the authority of the previous pastors. He was going to change all that. He lasted six months.

Sometimes the reason people are resisting is found in the life of the leader. At other times, it doesn't matter who the leader is, the problem of resistance is built into the people.

One example of resistance to authority happened in a church with which I am acquainted. The church had been established for about 25 years previous to its sale. During those 25 years the church had several pastors, none of whom was the authority.

One man who had invested great sums of money into the work from the beginning became a kind of spiritual godfather. He had the legal papers for the church in his home, and the keys to the building. What he said in the meetings of that church was considered to be right—no questions asked. When the church started to decline, no one realized that the problem was this man. They blamed it on different pastors. Finally, the church declined all the way down to this one man. Everyone else left. Sad.

This problem of authority is enormous, but very few want to deal with it, or to bring any understanding of it to the many Christian organizations that face it.

WHAT IS AUTHORITY?

Webster's dictionary lists the following meanings of the word "authority":

1. Legal or rightful power; a right to command or to act; jurisdiction.
2. A person, board or commission having power in a particular field.
3. Government; those exercising power or command.
4. One claimed, or appealed to, in support of opinions, actions, measures, etc; hence:
   a. Testimony; witness.
   b. A precedent; previous decision of a court.
   c. A book or its author.
   d. Justification; warrant.
5. Power due to opinion or esteem; influence of character, station, mental or moral superiority, or the like.

As these definitions are examined, they seem to describe

what most people would say about authority. The problem with all of these definitions deals with the source or basis of all authority. What is the ultimate authority? If a so-called "authority" must present its credentials to another individual, group or institution, it cannot be the ultimate authority. If our "right" to authority is given to us, then we are not the ultimate authority.

PROBLEMS IN SOCIETY THAT CAUSE RESISTANCE TO AUTHORITY

Today people question authority (and authorities) more than ever. Some say that our society has a "crisis in authority." There is a breakdown in authority and the exercising of it in every realm of society, including schools, churches, businesses and government (at all levels). There is little respect for authority, and the rights of the individual are exalted to the exclusion of authority which makes those rights possible in the first place.

What has gone wrong? Why are people not responding to authority? Why do most people question the right of authorities to rule and lead? Why do leaders have such a difficult time dealing with those under their leadership? Here are a few reasons people give.

Undisciplined Children
When there is no consistent pattern of discipline on the part of the parents toward their children, a spirit of rebellion develops. Proverbs 29:15 says, "The rod and reproof give wisdom, but a child who gets his own way brings shame to his mother." Proverbs 29:17 adds, "Correct your son, and he will give you comfort; he will also delight your soul." Proverbs 22:6 shows us the importance of the parental responsibility when it states: "Train up a child in

the way he should go, even when he is old he will not depart from it."

Proverbs 19:18 points out the need to discipline early: "Discipline your son while there is hope, and do not desire his death." Parents who argue that they love their children too much to discipline them are only proving the opposite. Proverbs 13:24 makes that clear: "He who spares his rod hates his son, but he who loves him disciplines him diligently."

The reason children need discipline is recorded in Proverbs 22:15: "Foolishness is bound up in the heart of a child; the rod of discipline will remove it far from him." One problem is that too many parents do not distinguish between *discipline* and *authority*. Perhaps the following chart will help us to see the difference, and how the discipline of children is related to their respect for and response to authority.

A child who grows up under the "punishment" concept will manifest a resistance to authority much more than the

	Discipline	Punishment
Purpose	To develop maturity by correction	To inflict penalty for an offense
Focus	Future correct deeds	Past misdeeds
Parents' Attitudes	Love/concern	Hostility/anger/ frustration
Child's Emotions	Security and trust	Fear and guilt
Child's Conduct	Submission/respect for authority	Rebellion against authority

one who is properly disciplined. The lack of any discipline can also prove damaging to the attitudes of the child in later life. If the parents give the child everything the child wants or demands, there is every possibility that there will be a resistance to authority later in the child's life.

A man came to my office one day to talk about one of his employees, who was a Christian but was failing to sub-

> *Without moral absolutes, there must inevitably be a breakdown in authority and people's response to it.*

mit to authority. This employer wanted to do the right thing. I had an opportunity to talk with the rebellious young man and discovered that he viewed his employer as though he were his father. His father never disciplined him, and in his childhood he always got his parents to respond by throwing a tantrum, or making a scene.

The young man had hostile attitudes toward his employer and was extremely upset that he could not get his own way at work as he had at home when he was growing up. My advice to him was to submit to authority or lose his job. He responded well, fortunately.

Many of the problems in leadership can be traced to improper discipline in the homes of the people who now must work together. The real solution to this problem is to go back to basics in the home. Teach and discipline according to God's Word.

The immediate problems at work can be solved only by the person's recognition of the problem and a willingness to be submissive to authority. That will take the power and control of the Holy Spirit. For a person to overcome years of improper discipline in his home is difficult, but not impossible. A pattern of submission to God and authority can overcome the pattern of resistance and rebellion.

Society's Failure to Teach Moral Absolutes

It is not difficult to understand how this problem affects the matter of authority. A relative standard of morality will lead one to a humanistic philosophy where the "self" is the authority and the one determining what is morally right or wrong.

Today's society, which says, "If it feels good, do it," has concluded that the person responsible for determining the morality of any word or action is none other than yourself! We are often told that if everyone agrees to it, then that makes it right. Or, if at least the majority has voted it, then it is right!

Without moral absolutes, there must inevitably be a breakdown in authority and people's response to it. An illustration of this can be found in Romans 10:3. Paul says, "For not knowing about God's righteousness, and seeking to establish their own, they did not subject themselves to the righteousness of God."

In the intellectual atmosphere of today's colleges and universities, every statement and axiom can be questioned. Nothing is ever regarded as being true or not true, right or wrong. The answer today is, "It all depends!" Morality is flexible, depending on the situation or condition of things involved.

The mood of most people is that they do not want anyone telling them what to do or that something *must* be done. That suggests a certain moral "oughtness," or requirement, and demands a moral authority behind it!

People say, "Who says so?" Or, "Who does he think he is?" Or, "What makes him think he is the authority around here?" The atmosphere of rebellion and resistance is thriving in what many call a "moral vacuum."

The Failure to Teach Principles of Authority

No doubt some of the blame can be placed on institutions of learning that have not taught correct principles of leadership and authority. Authority, leadership and management are subjects of great interest to many people, but the way these great subjects are taught in most institutions leaves many in doubt and question about assuming the role of leadership.

To be in a place of authority today involves much criticism and attack. In analyzing why this is true, many point to the way management courses are taught. The rights of the individual have been exalted to the point that those in authority always appear to be the "bad guys."

Attacks upon people in authority are frequent in college and university classrooms. Everyone seems to be "in it for themselves." People cheat and lie, and have no qualms about disobeying the law. If you can get away with it, it seems to be all right to do it. No wonder there is a crisis in authority today!

The Failure of Leaders to Be Good Examples

Scandals in the lives of those in authority have a tendency to weaken the people's response to authority. If a leader's life does not back up what he says, then he can hardly be trusted and relied upon in the matter of exercising his authority. This is certainly a valid criticism, and some of the blame must rest upon the shoulders of those in positions of authority.

Proverbs 29:2 says, "When the righteous increase, the

people rejoice, but when a wicked man rules, people groan." The New Testament places great emphasis upon the qualifications of those in positions of leadership—they are to be examples. Of course, such moral conduct assumes that there are moral absolutes upon which to make our evaluations and these absolutes have moral authority.

In speaking about false teachers and ungodly leaders, the Bible says:

> The Lord knows how to rescue the godly from temptation, and to keep the unrighteous under punishment for the day of judgment, and especially those who indulge the flesh in its corrupt desires and *despise authority* (2 Pet. 2:9-10; italics added).

Jude adds in verse 8 of his book: "Yet in the same manner these men, also by dreaming, defile the flesh, and *reject authority*" (italics added). It is a characteristic of these false teachers to despise and reject authority.

The Natural Tendency Toward Rebellion
Some do not like to admit or acknowledge this truth, but it is found in the Bible over and over again. Man is sinful, and his actions are controlled by a sinful and selfish nature with which he was born. David said in Psalm 51:5, "Behold, I was brought forth in iniquity, and in sin my mother conceived me." Ephesians 2:1-3 graphically portrays this problem:

> And you were dead in your trespasses and sins, in which you formerly walked according to the course of this world, according to the prince of the power of the air, of the spirit that is now working

in the sons of disobedience. Among them we too all formerly lived in the lusts of our flesh, indulging the desires of the flesh and of the mind, and were *by nature* children of wrath, even as the rest (emphasis mine).

First John 1:8 and 10 say: "If we say that we have no sin, we are deceiving ourselves, and the truth is not in us....If we say that we have not sinned, we make Him a liar, and His word is not in us." It seems very clear that the problem is not merely that of parents, authorities, institutions, standards of morality in society or anything that is outside of man. The problem is in our own hearts! We are rebels by nature! We are prone toward self and sin, not submission to godly authority.

We do not want anyone telling us what to do—it is against our nature! Paul describes the human dilemma:

For even though they knew God, they did not honor Him as God, or give thanks; but they became futile in their speculations, and their foolish heart was darkened. Professing to be wise, they became fools, and exchanged the glory of the incorruptible God for an image in the form of corruptible man and of birds and four-footed animals and crawling creatures (Rom. 1:21-23).

Romans 1:30 adds that by nature people are "slanderers, haters of God, insolent, arrogant, boastful, inventors of evil, disobedient to parents." In describing the last days, Paul tells us that men will be "boastful, arrogant, revilers, disobedient to parents" (2 Tim.3:1-5). Yes, the problem is in the human heart. We are sinners by nature and act.

In 1 Thessalonians 4:1-8, Paul describes God's principles and teaching concerning the practice of immorality. He includes a fascinating statement about rejecting authority in verse 8: "Consequently, he who rejects this is not rejecting man but the God who gives His Holy Spirit to you." The point here is that our rebellion and rejection is primarily directed toward God Himself.

> *Christian organizations can experience great disunity, disloyalty and rebellion to authority if the sin natures of those employed there are not controlled by the Holy Spirit.*

Thank God that there is a solution for the rebellion in the heart of all of us! Our sin has been paid for by the precious blood of Jesus Christ, and salvation is made possible through His work on the cross and His resurrection. It demands faith in what Christ has done for us, not in what we can do for Him. We must believe on the Lord Jesus Christ in order to be saved.

When we are "born again" we receive a new nature from God that is inclined toward Him. This new nature is in constant conflict with our old nature (which will not be removed until the coming of Christ). The understanding and response toward authority should be much greater among believers than among nonbelievers.

Of course believers can allow their old sin natures to dominate and become what the Bible calls "carnal." Christian organizations can experience great disunity, disloyalty and rebellion to authority if the sin natures of those employed there are not controlled by the Holy Spirit. The secret to an effective organization where there is response and respect toward authority is a Spirit-filled life. One part of the fruit of the Spirit is "self-control." When we are controlled by the Holy Spirit, we will not carry out the desires of the flesh (including rebellion and failure to submit to authority), according to Galatians 5:16.

ORGANIZATIONAL PROBLEMS THAT CAUSE RESISTANCE TO AUTHORITY

In addition to the basic problem of the old sin nature and the failures of parents, society, institutions, etc., there are some practical problems in every organization that can lead to authority problems. Spotting these early and doing something about them can save the leader many heartaches.

No Job Descriptions

When people do not know what to do, they get frustrated and resist authority. When the lines of responsibility are not clearly drawn in job descriptions, people have a tendency to get into one another's hair! There is overlapping, causing attitudes such as "That's not my job," or "Nobody told me to do that," or "That's your problem, not mine."

Job descriptions start at the top. Until we know what the chief leader is to do, we cannot design the jobs immediately under him.

A job description does not need to be lengthy or too detailed. It should deal with basics: what is expected, to whom responsible, for whom responsible, limits of authority, etc.

No Follow-through by the Leadership

This is a common complaint. When a person submits a request to the leadership and it is ignored or neglected, attitudes of resistance develop immediately. Leaders must learn to follow through on matters that affect their people.

One of our staff members was becoming resistant and it was starting to show. In dealing with the problem, I learned that I was the problem. He had submitted plans to me that had not been acted upon, nor had he been informed of what I was doing about it. He deserved to be upset. He should be submissive at all times, but his reaction was understandable.

No Explanations

When no explanations are given for decisions that affect the majority of people who work for you, attitudes of resistance begin to develop. Leaders must learn to share with people as to why they are doing what they are doing. Everyone will not agree, but they'll all be happy their opinions were heard and that the leader was willing to explain. When the people who work for you are the last ones to hear about decisions that are made, they feel neglected and that the leadership does not value them very highly.

It seemed like a simple matter—moving a few offices around, relocating people, and all without explanation. You guessed it—I had problems! I wound up explaining in some detail to every person involved in the moves! It was my fault, not theirs. Though the matter seemed small to me, it was not at all inconsequential to them.

Showing Partiality

This will do it every time! Just start paying one staff member more than another at the same level, and you'll see some resistance to authority. Give one staff member a nicer office than another who serves at the same level of responsibility, and you'll have problems, unless everyone is agreeable, loving and willing. Of course, if your offices are all different, then you'll have to make some decisions that won't please everybody, but taking time to talk it over can sure help!

Showing partiality can be seen in the amount of time spent by the leader with a particular staff person, especially when it's not company business. People are very sensitive, and leaders must be understanding toward how the people feel. Leaders must show love and concern for all, without partiality.

Demanding Extra Work Without Asking

When a leader simply tells an employee what he wants them to do and it is not a part of the person's regular job, an attitude of resistance can easily develop. The employee begins to feel the leader does not really care or understand his feelings. Naturally, employees should be willing to submit to the employer's demands (the Bible teaches this), but spiritual leaders will do themselves a favor if they stop demanding and begin asking.

If a leader needs an employee to stay and work extra hours, he should ask, not demand. A question like, "Would it be possible for you to help me complete this by staying after work today?" is much better than "You'll have to stay after work today to complete this project." When the leader wants an employee to do work that is not a part of that person's job, it's better to say, "Would you be able to help me on this; I know it's not your job, but I really need help!" than to say, "Have this done as soon as you can!"

The leader who works like this is building for the future. People will respond more quickly to your needs when they know you are asking, not demanding. Maybe you have a right to demand; but if you think about it, the level of productivity might be higher when there is an atmosphere of love and kindness.

One final thing about this: Make sure you express your sincere thanks for the extra effort. Gratefulness leads to better response. One of the most forgotten forms of worker compensation is the phrase, "Thank you very much." It means much more than money!

Organizational problems can cause resistance to authority. Don't let them continue. Learn to deal with them quickly. People respond to leaders who care about them and their feelings.

☑ LEADER'S CHECKLIST

1. Do certain people resist your authority? Who are they? Have you discovered why?
2. How would you handle someone who resisted your authority?
3. Is your example before others such that people can respond favorably to your authority? Why?
4. Do you have an adequate job description for yourself? For your co-workers? Are these in writing?
5. Do you always respond immediately to the requests of others?
6. Do you take time to explain your decisions when they affect others? Describe a recent situation when you did this.
7. Do you ever show partiality? Name a recent instance.
8. Do you have a habit of demanding rather than asking? What is the difference?

14

HOW DO YOU GET AUTHORITY?

AUTHORITY is essential to the effective operation of any organization. It exists whether it is recognized or not. It often lies in a corner unnoticed by those with titles and offices. How does a person get authority? Where does it come from?

THE BASIS OF AUTHORITY

The foundation of all authority is God. Without God, there is no moral foundation for authority. Without God, it is impossible to establish moral rightness. Everything is relative and situational without God. There are no absolutes without God.

God as the Source of Authority

Before anything else existed, there was God. The Bible does not set out to prove His existence, it assumes it. The One who created us has the right to tell us what to do. Every authority in the world is accountable for the exercise of that authority to God Himself. Many management problems could be cleared up if this principle were recognized and applied.

The Bible teaches that God is king over all and His Kingdom includes everything and everyone (see Dan. 4:3,34; 6:26; 7:14). King David said that God was the head over all, and that He rules over all (see 1 Chron. 29:11,12). Everything comes from Him.

Romans 9:21 says He is the potter and we are the clay; He has a right to form us the way He wants. Psalm 24 reminds us that the earth and all it contains belong to the Lord. Romans 11:36 says all things come from Him, are being worked through Him and have Him as their ultimate goal. Psalm 103:19 tells us that God's sovereignty rules over all.

Levels of Authority Revealed in the Word

God has also determined the levels of authority that exist in society. God the Father gave special authority to His Son, Jesus Christ (see John 17:2). Christ's authority affects many areas of our lives. In marriage, Christ is the head of every husband, and the husband the head of his wife. In the Church, Christ is the head. In business, employers are reminded of their Master in heaven (see Eph. 6:9).

God's authority is expressed clearly in the written pages of the Bible, making the Bible the number one manual on authority. The Bible rings with authority in statements like "Thus says the Lord" and "The Word of the Lord came to me, saying." The Bible demands our obedience and submission to what it says. The reason it can do that is because it is God's Word. God is the ultimate source of all authority.

One of the major problems in establishing the principle of authority in a person's life is his relationship to God. If he does not recognize God as the ultimate source of all authority, he will see no need of submitting to levels of authority which God in His Word has established.

Submitting to Authority

God has established authority in marriage, family, government, business and the church. The believer is exhort-

> *If you cannot submit to authority yourself, you cannot expect others to submit to you.*

ed to submit to the authorities that God has established.

One of the keys to having authority is learning to submit. It almost seems to be an axiom that the degree of authority in a person's life is directly traceable to the amount of submission to the authorities which God has placed in that person's life. If you cannot submit to authority yourself, you cannot expect others to submit to you. God promises to exalt the one who learns to submit (see Jas. 4:10).

Much of the problem in responding to authority lies in the mistaken ideas people have about authority. These ideas often control a person's response even though he is unaware of it.

MISTAKEN IDEAS OF AUTHORITY

Some of the problems people have in working well with others and being under the leadership of others are due to mistaken ideas of authority they have been accustomed to. Following are some of these mistaken ideas.

Authority from an Inner Feeling
We often speak of "authoritarian" figures—people who seem to have innate authority. They feel it, and others around them feel the same thing. This authority can arise from the way people talk, dress or relate to others.

But this is imaginary authority, not real. It is imagined by the individual himself or others around him. It sometimes results from a sense of pride and self-confidence. It can also stem from insecurity which causes the person to manifest authoritarian attitudes and actions. How long and loudly we talk sometimes reveals our insecurity and pride.

Authority by Right of Ownership
This mistaken idea assumes that the exercise of authority can be learned or acquired by the individual who aspires to it. People who believe this will spend time reading and studying the principles of management and authority, believing that this knowledge gives them the right or the ability to exercise authority over others.

Sometimes this mistaken idea is based on that which a person has bought or inherited. There is a very real sense in which he who owns is he who has authority. However, merely owning cannot guarantee effective authority—especially in the matter of spiritual leadership. You may have the power that money can bring, but it does not mean that you have spiritual leadership or authority.

Authority Based on the Will of the Majority
This common belief represents the "democratic" way of doing things. The trouble is that voting someone into a

position of authority does not, of itself, bring that authority. If 100 people vote for a leader and 51 say yes and 49 say no, the person is elected. This particular example reveals the danger of this method of establishing authority.

To compensate for this problem, many religious organizations insist on a two-thirds majority in selecting leaders. This, too, is no guarantee that a spiritual leader has been chosen or that spiritual authority will be exercised.

This method is often based on popularity or the person who is best known and offers the least problems. In order for this process to be used, other factors, to be discussed shortly, must be considered first. It is very possible for the majority to be wrong. When people are not Spirit-filled or living godly lives or basing their opinions on biblical standards, it will be very difficult for them to make the right decisions.

Authority Based on Acceptance
This view contains a very important truth: When no one responds to an individual's authority, there will be questions about that person's ability to manage or rule. But the failure of people to respond is no guarantee that a person is not a leader.

A wife is to respond to her husband's authority regardless of whether he is properly exercising it. This is true of the responsibility of children to parents, employees to employers, etc. The problem may rest with the attitudes of those under that authority. Their past record of subjection may also affect their response to authority.

Many leaders are looking to those under them for assurance of their position and authority. This kind of leader is extremely insecure and will continue to be so until he discovers the real basis of authority. He will have a tendency to compromise and tolerate situations that ought not to exist simply because he does not want to offend people under him, people whose response brings him assurance of his authority.

Authority Based on Office or Title

This is so prevalent in society today, one wonders when it is going to be challenged and buried. It appeals to human pride to have a particular title or office and thus feel impor-

---

The size of an office or its elaborate furnishings is often the way people determine the "executives." This is foolish, and in no way represents real authority!

---

tant and authoritative. But all the lofty titles in the world cannot give you the authority that God describes in His Word.

Promotion is a key motivating factor in the business world today, especially when a larger salary and greater benefits are involved. Sometimes we let these "crutches" support us in believing we have a measure of authority. But real authority is based on different principles.

It is important at times to have titles that represent the work a person does, but when they are used to give the person a sense of authority, it is a waste of time. Real authority does not come by merely giving a person a title. Nor does it come by the kind of office he has or his physical surroundings. The size of an office or its elaborate furnishings is often the way people determine the "executives." This is foolish, and in no way represents real authority!

It is not a bad idea for executives to move offices from time to time to teach this principle. It is also a good idea for an executive to give his office to a person with less authority and take a smaller office for himself. If more executives would do this, there would be fewer problems of interpersonal relationships and more understanding of what real authority is all about. Maybe those who design offices (especially in Christian organizations) should make them all identical in size and furnishings!

THE TRUE BASIS OF SPIRITUAL AUTHORITY

Spiritual authority is based on factors that God Himself reveals in His written Word. Your ability to have great influence upon the lives of others is dependent upon these factors. The influence that God wants you to accomplish and exercise toward others is built upon what you, as a person, are really like.

Your reputation is what people think you are; your character is what God knows you to be. More could be said about these factors, and no doubt more factors could be added to this list. Hopefully, these few principles will guide all of us into a true understanding of authority.

Submission to God Himself

James 4:7 says, "Submit therefore to God." Verse 10 says, "Humble yourselves in the presence of the Lord, and He will exalt you." The way up is the way down! Humility and submission are the true foundation of of spiritual authority. The amount of spiritual authority in our lives is directly in proportion to our humility and submission to God and His Word.

There will be many tests along the way to see what our submission to God is like. There will be times when we will be tempted to compromise or violate God's Word for a moment's pleasure or profit. Those times are the keys to the spiritual authority we will exercise. If we are not submissive to God, the chances are that those under our authority will not submit to us.

A Godly Life-style

Hebrews 13:7 says, "Remember those who led you, who spoke the word of God to you; and considering the result of their conduct, imitate their faith." Notice that the response of the followers to what the leaders say is based on the conduct of those leaders. The concept of "Practice what you preach" is constantly emphasized in the Scriptures. Leaders who cannot be trusted and respected in terms of godly life-style will have very little spiritual authority in the lives of others.

Paul wrote in 1 Thessalonians 1:5, "For our gospel did not come to you in word only, but also in power and in the Holy Spirit and with full conviction; just as you know what kind of men we proved to be among you for your sake." He said further:

> For our exhortation does not come from error or impurity or by way of deceit; but just as we have been approved by God to be entrusted with the gospel, so we speak, not as pleasing men but God, who examines our hearts. For we never came with flattering speech, as you know, nor with a pretext for greed—God is witness—nor did we seek glory from men, either from you or from others, even though as apostles of Christ we might have asserted our authority (1 Thess. 2:3-6).

Your Love for People

People respond best to loving authority. Children respond to the authority of parents when it is backed by love and concern. Discipline without love can produce rebellion rather than submission. In 1 Thessalonians 2:3-12, Paul spoke about his authority and influence among these believers. In contrasting his style with the wrong motives of others, he said:

> But we proved to be gentle among you, *as a nursing mother tenderly cares for her own children.* Having thus a fond affection for you, we were well-pleased to impart to you not only the gospel of God but also our own lives, because you had become very dear to us.... Just as you know how we were exhorting and encouraging and imploring each one of you *as a father would his own children* (vv. 7,8,11, italics added).

Your loving concern for others will increase your authority and influence in their lives.

A Servant's Heart

Jesus referred to the kind of authority that the rulers of the Gentiles use. In Mark 10:42 He spoke of how they "lord it over them." But His kind of spiritual authority is different:

> But it is not so among you, but whoever wishes to become great among you shall be your servant; and whoever wishes to be first among you shall be slave of all. For even the Son of Man did not come to be served, but to serve, and to give His life a ransom for many (vv. 43-45).

Our desire and willingness to serve others are keys to our spiritual authority. Spiritual leaders will seek to make those who work under them more effective. They will serve them in every way possible. They will try to make conditions and situations affecting their work as pleasant as possible. They will give them opportunities and challenges to grow and develop under their leadership without trying to suppress that growth for selfish reasons.

Ways to Get Authority

Spiritual authority is the most important kind of authority. This does not mean that other kinds of authorities are not important or real. A husband is the authority in his marriage. That is real authority, but not necessarily spiritual authority. A wife is to respond to her husband's authority even when he is not obeying God's Word (see 1 Pet. 3:1-6). However, her response and his blessing will be so much better when the husband's authority is also spiritual authority, based on the principles we have just shared.

So, in what ways can a person get authority? These thoughts are very practical and come out of the arena of personal experience. They are in addition to what was said about spiritual authority. When we are placed into positions of authority in any one of these areas or through any one of these ways, we should then seek to have spiritual authority in all we do and say.

By Making Decisions

When you decide to get married, you (if a man) automatically become the authority in your marriage. It is a position which God has previously established. When you decide to have children, you automatically become the authority as a parent. When you decide to apply for a job, and you are hired, a measure of authority accompanies the job you have received.

By Delegation from Others

When your employer gives you authority, it comes to you by delegation. Your authority exists because of his authority. The way you use it may determine the extent of your authority in the lives of others, but nonetheless, you have a measure of authority because it was given to you.

By Establishing a Ministry

Whenever a person develops something from the beginning, it is his baby. Authority exists because he brought it into existence. He must make the decisions as to the transfer of authority to others. This is a matter of prior claim. He has a claim upon that ministry because he began it.

When an attempt is made to change the authority in an organization or particular ministry without the consent of the one who founded it, inevitably there are problems. It is better to start a new ministry than to change the old without approval of the one who started it.

This truth applies to a group as well as an individual. When a group establishes a brand new ministry, and another group comes along and tries to change things, immediately there is conflict and deep problems in authority. Organizations can be changed when the authority is properly transferred. Otherwise, a new ministry must be established.

Through Financial Support

This can be a dangerous problem in authority. Money does buy power, whether we like it or not. A wise leader will do all he can to keep people from exercising authority because of financial support.

Still, if you bought something with your own money, then the purchase grants you a measure of authority over that item. The principle of private property is involved here. If you buy a piece of land it belongs to you, then you have the authority in determining the future of it.

In Christian ministry, believers must be careful to support God's work with their financial resources without desiring authority in the use of their money. Charitable contributions should have no strings attached.

A gift is not a right to exercise authority. A gift should be based on love, not a desire to control another person or organization.

Through Personal Experience

If you have had great experience in some area of ministry, you will be looked to for advice and expertise. You become an authority because you know what you are talking about.

It becomes a problem when your experience becomes the final word. When you are not open to new ideas, your past experience can irritate people rather than help them. Statements like, "It won't work; we tried that before!" or "We've always done it this way!" can seriously endanger your authority before others.

Experiences can deepen your authority when you apply them to new situations in ways that are wise and helpful. The more your past experience helps those in the present, the greater will be your authority.

Remember, the greatest authority is spiritual authority. Make sure that the authority you concentrate on is that which produces spiritual results and gives glory to God.

☑Leader's Checklist

1. Have you properly established your relationship to God as the ultimate source of all authority? Describe how you see this happening.
2. Is submitting to God's authority a problem in your life?
3. Review the section "Mistaken Ideas of Authority." Do you recognize any of these problems in your life? Which ones need your immediate attention?
4. On a scale of 1-10 how do you rate yourself in being submissive to God?

   1   2   3   4   5   6   7   8   9   10
   Rebellious   Submissive

5. On a scale of 1-10 how do you rate yourself on having a godly life-style?

   1   2   3   4   5   6   7   8   9   10
   Worldly life-style   Godly life-style

6. Do you really love the people you lead? How are they able to tell?
7. How willing are you to be a servant to others?
8. Review the section "Ways to Get Authority." If you are in a position of authority, how did you get there?
9. Do you give glory to God for spiritual results?

15
How to Respond to Authority

MANY reasons could be given as to why it is difficult to respond to a leader's authority. It is especially easy to list such difficulties when we are reluctant to face the responsibility to submit and respond to authority. For example, it is difficult to respond when a leader...

1. Tries to dominate and intimidate you.
2. Must always be right.
3. Wants to use and abuse you however he desires.
4. Does not care what happens to you.
5. Believes that fancy offices, big salaries, and important-sounding titles give a person authority and respect.
6. Never shows appreciation for what you have done.
7. Doesn't know your name.
8. Takes the credit for what others have done.
9. Plays favorites and discriminates.
10. Lies to you and deceives others.

The list could go on. Many leaders do not deserve the willing submission of those who work under them or for them. But is that a reason or justification for our lack of response to their authority?

Andy was having a difficult time at work. His boss constantly threatened him, and Andy never seemed to be able to please his boss in the projects he was assigned to do. Andy developed a bitter spirit toward his boss and began openly to criticize him. In little, and sometimes big, ways, Andy was showing his rebellion. The feared day arrived. It was on Friday afternoon, the typical day for employers to dismiss an employee.

Andy was surprised, not at being fired, but at the reason. His boss confronted him about his so-called Christian commitment, and reminded him of the Bible's teaching about submission to authority. His boss told him that unless he changed his ways, he would continue to have trouble no matter where he was employed.

Andy was surprised because he had no idea that his boss had any connections with Christianity or any knowledge of what the Bible teaches. Fortunately for Andy, he received some good counsel from a trusted Christian friend, and began to see the issue of submission to authority as it was affecting his life and attitudes.

What Does the Bible Teach About Submission?

Authority comes from God. He does not always commend the actions of the person in authority, but He honors the position of authority and requires believers to do the same. This issue is brought out in Romans 13:1-7 in a powerful way:

> Let every person be in subjection to the govern-

ing authorities. For there is no authority except from God, and those which exist are established by God. Therefore he who resists authority has opposed the ordinance of God; and they who have opposed will receive condemnation upon themselves. For rulers are not a cause of fear for good behavior, but for evil. Do you want to have no fear of authority? Do what is good, and you will have praise from the same; for it is a minister of God to you for good. But if you do what is evil, be afraid; for it does not bear the sword for nothing; for it is a minister of God, an avenger who brings wrath upon the one who practices evil. Wherefore it is necessary to be in subjection, not only because of wrath, but also for conscience' sake. For because of this you also pay taxes, for rulers are servants of God, devoting themselves to this very thing. Render to all what is due them: tax to whom tax is due; custom to whom custom; fear to whom fear; honor to whom honor.

The Bible is clear: "Let every person be in subjection to the governing authorities." Paul again writes: "Remind them to be subject to rulers, to authorities, to be obedient, to be ready for every good deed, to malign no one, to be uncontentious, gentle, showing every consideration for all men" (Titus 3:1,2). Again the message is clear. And First Peter 2:13-17 contains the same message:

Submit yourselves for the Lord's sake to every human institution, whether to a king as the one in authority, or to governors as sent by him for the punishment of evildoers and the praise of those who do right. For such is the will of God that by doing right you may silence the ignorance of foolish men. Act as free men, and do not use your freedom as a covering for evil, but use it as bondslaves of God. Honor all men; love the brotherhood, fear God, honor the king.

Again, we are to "submit" to authority, both in terms of the people in positions of authority from the king on down to those who carry out his purposes, as well as in

---

Submission will bring God's reward....Though no one else sees your willing submission to authority, God does.

---

terms of laws and institutions that authorities have established. Pay taxes, honor leaders, submit to authority—the message is clear.

The only exception would be when human authority violates the authority of God. According to Acts 5:29, Peter and the other apostles had to resist and suffer the consequences when confronted by human authority telling them to disobey the clear instruction of God. They said, "We must obey God rather than men."

Submission is a principle governing all areas of our lives. In marriage, spouses are to submit to each other, wives to husbands and husbands to wives (Eph. 5:21-33; Col. 3:18). In the family, children are told to obey their parents, and that this is right and well-pleasing to the Lord (Eph. 6:1-2; Col. 3:20). Believers are told to obey their leaders in the church (Hebrews 13:17), as well as in society.

Submission recognizes that authority is ordained of God and obeys because of this, even when you think the authority is wrong. If it does not violate the authority of God, we are to submit even when we do not agree. It is not our natural tendency to submit and respond to authority. We think we are right or have a better way of doing things. We question, challenge, criticize, resist and rebel. It's our nature to do so. We need to be controlled by the Holy Spirit!

WHY SHOULD WE SUBMIT TO AUTHORITY?

For one thing, because the Lord commanded it. If we love Him, we will keep His commandments (see John 14:15). The reasons that follow all flow out of obedience to the Lord's command. If we do not understand "why," we are still to obey God, trusting Him completely for the reasons and the results.

It Pleases the Lord

That was the message God gave to children in obeying their parents—"this is well-pleasing to the Lord" (Col. 3:20). Wives are told that submission is "fitting in the Lord" (Col. 3:18). Submission is godly behavior, it reflects the Lord's control in our lives and He is honored through it.

It Is Right

Ephesians 6:1 tells children to obey their parents because "this is right." God determines what is right and what is wrong. It is not up to debate or discussion on our part. We are to do right no matter what we think, feel or desire.

Romans 13:5-7 tells us that one of the reasons we are to submit to authority is "for conscience' sake." This is why we pay taxes to support the authorities. Because God has commanded us to do so, and because it is the right thing to do, then we must obey in order to have a clear conscience—and that includes paying our taxes!

Submission Leads to Long and Productive Lives

Ephesians 6:3 tells children that their obedience comes with a promise: "That it may be well with you, and that you may live long on the earth."

It Keeps Us from Serious Consequences

Romans 13:4-5 makes it clear that if we do wrong and resist the authority then the authority has been given the right by God to bring consequences. The authority is called "a minister of God, an avenger who brings wrath." Therefore we are instructed to be in subjection to authority "because of wrath."

It Protects the Testimony of the Word

In Titus 2:5, wives are to be "subject to their own husbands, that the word of God may not be dishonored." The Bible obviously teaches a wife to be submissive to her husband. If she is not, then the Word of God is discredited and dishonored by her behavior. In Titus 2:9, slaves are told to be "subject to their own masters in everything" and the reason given, "that they may adorn the doctrine of God our Savior in every respect."

Submission Is the Will of God

Peter makes this point clear in 1 Peter 2:15—"For such is the will of God that by doing right you may silence the ignorance of foolish men." People often look for something to criticize in the life-style of the believer. If they hated our Lord Jesus, you know that they will hate us (John 15:18-21). When we are submissive to authority, it puts them to silence; they have nothing to criticize or attack.

Slaves are told in Ephesians 6:5-7 to be obedient to their masters, and that they are to do "the will of God from the heart." It is the will of God to be submissive, but we are urged to make it an inward commitment and desire, not simply an outward performance.

Obedience Wins Others to the Lord

First Peter 3:1-6 gives us excellent teaching regarding a wife's submission to a husband who does not obey the Word. She can win him "without a word" by her submissive behavior. God calls it "the imperishable quality of a gentle and quiet spirit, which is precious in the sight of God" (v. 4). Submission "adorns" or "beautifies" the person and makes them attractive.

It Brings Grace from the Lord

First Peter 5:5 says: "You younger men, likewise, be subject to your elders; and all of you, clothe yourselves with humility toward one another, for God is opposed to the proud, but gives grace to the humble."

It is humbling to submit to others, but God will exalt you. God gives special "grace" to those who submit.

Submission Brings Reward from the Lord

The apostle Paul wrote:

> Slaves, be obedient to those who are your masters according to the flesh, with fear and trembling, in the sincerity of your heart, as to Christ; not by way of eyeservice, as men-pleasers, but as slaves of Christ, doing the will of God from the heart. With good will render service, as to the Lord, and not to men, knowing that whatever good thing each one

does, this he will receive back from the Lord,
whether slave or free (Eph. 6:5-8).

Submission will bring God's reward—"he will receive
back from the Lord." Though no one else sees your willing
submission to authority, God does. Colossians 3:22-25 contains the same insight:

> Slaves, in all things obey those who are your mas-
> ters on earth, not with external service, as those
> who merely please men, but with sincerity of
> heart, fearing the Lord. Whatever you do, do your
> work heartily, as for the Lord rather than for men;
> knowing that from the Lord you will receive the
> reward of the inheritance. It is the Lord Christ
> whom you serve. For he who does wrong will
> receive the consequences of the wrong which he
> has done, and that without partiality.

"From the Lord you will receive the reward...." One day
we will hear (Lord willing) our Lord's words, "Well done
good and faithful servant." Speaking of His return, our
Lord promises, "Behold, I am coming quickly, and My
reward is with Me" (Rev. 22:12).

HOW TO SUBMIT TO AUTHORITY

Two words describe it: obey and do it! As we have seen, in
Colossians 3:22 slaves (employees) are told to obey their
masters (employers). It covers "all things." Nothing is left
out. We are told "Whatever you do, do your work hearti-
ly, as for the Lord rather than for men." Our attitudes are
extremely important.

On the negative side, we are warned about working to

please men, doing what we do because we are being watched or observed. Our reputation is what people think we are; our character is what God knows us to be. Our character is best understood in the dark, when no one else is around or will ever know. That's what we are.

On the positive side, we are to work with "sincerity of heart." The word "sincerity" is from a Greek word meaning single, in contrast to the word double. It means we have no hidden agenda; we are not hypocritical. We have a single purpose and desire—to glorify God and be submissive in our work and to those in authority over us. Wholeheartedness is based on our commitment to the Lord. We are serving the Lord, not merely those in authority over us.

☑ LEADER'S CHECKLIST

1. Why do some people resist authority?
2. List some reasons why certain people in positions of authority do not deserve the submission of those who work for them or under them.
3. What reasons can you give for submission to authority?
4. Why is submitting to authority the will of God?
5. How can a person "adorn the doctrine of God"?
6. List ways in which you can personally demonstrate your submission to authority.
7. Describe your attitude about paying taxes, and what you could do to be more pleasing to the Lord.
8. What are some things to avoid when submitting to authority?
9. When is it ever right to resist human authority?

LAW VI

STRATEGY:
You Need to Know Where You Are Going

16

GOOD LEADERS
HAVE A STRATEGY

AIM at nothing, and you'll hit it every time! We've all
heard that from time to time, but its truth sinks into
the hearts of very few, unfortunately! Do you know
where you're going? Leaders must have a strategy. They
must know how to get things done.

A good strategy is composed of:

1. *Objectives*—the basic purposes of the organization.
2. *Goals*—the specific ways in which the purposes of
   the organization will be measured and accomplished.
3. *Priorities*—the factors that determine when and why
   things are done.
4. *Planning*—the process used to achieve the goals
   (includes personnel, resources, obstacles and evaluation).
5. *Guidelines*—the moral and ethical framework in
   which the organization will seek to accomplish its
   goals.

Organizations should have a philosophy of ministry which includes these five elements. Every leader within that organization should be reminded of these things frequently. It is so easy to get sidetracked and off the main objectives and specific goals. It is the leader's responsibility to keep things on the right track.

WHY DO WE NEED A STRATEGY?

Many organizations and leaders are operating without a good strategy. They have only one goal in mind and that is to keep the organization going from day to day. They deal only with present problems and needs. Organizations like that have "a terminal illness." If not "terminal" it is at least "sick." An organization is not healthy that does not know where it is going and why.

Consider some of the reasons why you need a good strategy. Perhaps they will uncover some basic causes for frustration, confusion and lack of enthusiasm and growth within your organization.

In Order to Know *Why*

An organization may provide employment for people and may design specific jobs for people to do. But, if a strategy is missing, a person's reason for working diminishes. This is especially true in Christian organizations. There is a certain idealism in the heart of every believer who goes to work for a Christian organization. That person wants to be a part of something really great, something that will count for eternity. He or she likes to feel that the work is being done for the Lord.

And rightly so. At some point, when the Christian worker begins to ask why a certain thing is being done, the strategy is then vital. An explanation is needed. The worker needs to be motivated by the high and lofty goals of the organization. Otherwise, why not get another job in a secular institution (the pay is probably better anyway)?

One of our secretaries was discouraged. We chatted together one day about her work. She had lost sight of

> *The chain of command should be described so that the individual worker has no doubt as to how things can get done and through whom they must go for approval.*

how what she was doing fit into the important objectives and goals of the church. When she was reminded of them, tears came to her eyes. She realized the importance of her work once again. She was grateful to be a part of it. It wasn't the money that motivated her. I learned an important lesson.

To Maintain Interest
Without objectives and goals in an organization, it is easy to lose interest. It becomes more difficult to go into the office each day. Work is not exciting anymore. It's boring and dull. You begin to feel apathetic, indifferent to pressing needs and responsibilities. When this happens, the leader should take a good look at the strategy. Is there one? What does it say? Is it up-to-date?

One of our staff members was losing interest in a particular area of ministry. It was obvious to everyone around him. He knew the overall strategy of the organization, but he had not applied that to his area of ministry. Attendance had been declining in recent months. When reminded again of the importance of a strategy in every area of ministry, he immediately regained his interest. He wrote out a strategy for ministry, became enthusiastic and had new joy in serving the Lord.

In Order to Know What to Do

A pastor visited me one day from a nearby city. He was new, fresh out of seminary. He took the pastorate of a small church that had been struggling for several years. He proceeded to ask me some basic questions about what pastors should do. He said that he sat in his office day after day and nothing was happening. No one came by to see him. No one called him. He was bored and had nothing to do.

Frankly, I had a hard time identifying with this young man! But I realized that he was serious, and that he had no strategy. When I told him our strategy and gave him some ideas, he was overwhelmed. He didn't realize there was so much to do!

A common complaint in Christian organizations (that often goes unnoticed by the leadership) is that people don't know what to do. They have time on their hands. They don't know the overall strategy or how it applies to them in their area of ministry.

In Order to Know *How*

Strategy includes planning. Planning involves the "how" of an organization. Strategies for personnel, resources, etc., tell us how to arrive at the goals we want to accomplish. Organizations that have no strategy make it difficult for the people who work for them to accomplish things.

In a large organization it seems as though the channels

through which you must go to accomplish something are endless. It has been my observation that a person can work for the organization for a considerable length of time and still not know how to get things done in the most efficient manner. A strategy should help. In that strategy, the process by which something is accomplished should be clearly outlined. The chain of command should be described so that the individual worker has no doubt as to how things can get done and through whom they must go for approval.

Having said all of that, experience reminds me that the process by which things are done needs to be upgraded constantly and brought before the people involved in the organization. Staff changes can affect the process. Equipment can easily break down. Supplies can run out. Schedules can be changed. All of this demands communication with workers. Reminders must come often as to how things can and should be done.

To Evaluate Our Work

This may be the reason why so many leaders fail to have a strategy. We don't want to be evaluated by any form of measurement. It is too simple to spot weaknesses and failures in the organization. But, evaluation must go on. A leader's task is to evaluate constantly, cutting back on unproductive areas, and adding supplies and people to promising areas of growth.

I asked a pastor friend, "How are things going in your church?" He said, "I have no idea." He was honest, but after a few moments of discussion I learned he had no strategy. He did not know what his objectives were; he thus had no goals, or plans. No wonder he did not know how things were going in his own church!

The greatest danger in evaluation is when you compare

your work with someone else. There is no need to do that. You set the strategy for your church, and stick with it! Don't worry about what the other person in another organization is doing! The question is, are you achieving the goals which you have set for your ministry? If you are, praise the Lord! That's what counts! God is not evaluating us on the basis of what someone else has done!

To Exercise Spiritual Leadership

With our mouths we may profess to be committed to high and lofty purposes, but without a clearly-defined strategy, there's no real commitment to those purposes. A strategy suggests a certain seriousness about our spiritual leadership. We must know where we are going and how we are going to get there.

Musical chairs in the ministry is common. Pastors move quickly from one church to another, with each church suffering in the process. They are supposed to be spiritual leaders, but where are they going? A well-defined strategy will stop the constant changing of pastorates. It takes time to develop a strategy. Happy the Christian organization that has a strategy which demands a long-term leadership.

One pastor friend saw that his constant moves from church to church was directly related to the lack of goals and objectives in his ministry. As soon as he wrote them down on paper, he caught a vision of a long-term pastorate, and has settled down into a successful one at the present time.

To Carry Us Through Times of Crisis

A strategy will help you to be patient when things take a turn for the worse. When that slump hits, your strategy can sustain you. There will be temporary setbacks along the way, but your strategy helps you to put them in proper perspective.

A pastor from a nearby city called one day to tell me he was quitting his ministry in that church. The church was in a period of decline and he wanted out before it was too late, whatever that meant. I encouraged him to stay. (The words "I quit" ought to be removed from the spiritual leader's vocabulary!) He failed to take my advice (happens a lot), but has lived to regret it. He feels now that he made a mistake. His problem? He had no strategy—no goals or objectives.

It happens so often, you'd think leaders would respond and write out that strategy! However, human nature being what it is, many leaders continue to ignore this most basic fact of leadership—you must know where you are going if people are going to follow you!

HOW MUCH OF YOUR LIFE IS AFFECTED BY STRATEGY?

Once you understand what a strategy is and why it is so important, every area of your life is included in your strategy. Actually, there are three basic areas affected by your strategy: your personal life, your family life and your organizational life.

Personal objectives must be established and goals developed. A quick look at those personal goals will reveal many of the frustrations that a leader can feel. He can easily be frustrated in his life because he is not achieving any personal objectives and goals that he may have for himself.

For example, a leader may have a personal objective of keeping in excellent physical condition. He may set a goal of exercising twice a week. If his work schedule does not allow for this personal goal to be achieved he will become frustrated and in some cases the quality of his work can diminish.

To the believer, family goals are priorities. To spend time each week with your marital partner or your children is a must. It is most discouraging and damaging when these goals cannot be achieved. Leaders will do well to pay more attention to personal and family goals. They may

> *Goals often reflect our confidence and faith in a sovereign God. Do we trust Him to perform His work in us?*

discover roots of frustration and disappointment that presently affect their job.

Organizational goals must be established within the framework of priorities, especially as it relates to personal and family goals. A person's job is not more important than his family. But, achieving a balance between each of these areas—personal, family, and organizational—is not always easy.

During the first years of our marriage, my wife and I tried to establish the importance of our relationship by spending at least one evening together alone. We kept our date night faithfully. Later we changed to one day together (while the kids were in school). Every week we look forward to our one day together. It has helped us to establish the priority of one family goal we have—to stay best friends by being alone together at least one day a week. It's measurable, so it's a goal. The objective is to be best friends. Adjustments have to be made from time to time, but they are few and far between.

The reason why this family goal is important to me is because of what I know the Bible teaches about marriage and my personal need for companionship and love. It's also important because of its effect upon my job. I work better and more efficiently when I have time alone with my wife. When things are right between us, my work becomes much more enjoyable.

WHY IS GOAL-SETTING SO IMPORTANT?

It is impossible to determine the effectiveness of your life if you don't set goals. It is my opinion that everyone has goals. They may not write them down or even be able to communicate them to others, but they have them just the same. If you could penetrate a person's inner feelings and discover his goals, you could tell much about that person and his chances for productivity.

Unrealistic Goals

Sometimes the goals we set are unrealistic. They do not carefully evaluate the potential of people and resources. For example, it is unrealistic for a church in a community of 10,000 people isolated by 100 miles from any other community, to set a goal of 20,000 people as members of that church! It may not be unrealistic to set a goal like that in a major metropolitan area.

Unspecific Goals

On the other hand, the goals we have may not be attainable because they are not specific. A goal to reach as many people as possible with the gospel of Christ is really not a goal, but a fine purpose or objective. A specific goal within that objective might be to share the gospel door-to-door with 10,000 homes in your community in a three-month period of time.

Some do not like goals at all. What about the sovereignty of God? Well, God is sovereign all right, and He is running things in the universe. However, He does it through people. He ordains the means as well as the end. We are responsible to Him. Goals often reflect our confidence and faith in a sovereign God. Do we trust Him to perform His work in us?

Keeping Numbers in Perspective

The so-called "numbers game" is where the problem of goals is usually fought. To have a bigger attendance this week than last week is a goal, but it might be unworthy of believers committed to biblical principles.

Our goals are sometimes based on a carnal motive of comparison with others. The only One to whom we are accountable is God. Contests, prizes, competition and awards are often used to stimulate people toward the achieving of certain goals. Without getting into an argument over the validity of such methods in Christian organizations, we can at least emphasize the underlying motive of such methods. If the methods do not violate God's Word and if the motive is worthy and biblical, then the use of the methods must be allowable. You may not want to use any of those methods, but for some, they may be permissible.

Learn this truth: It is unwise to develop goals based upon comparison with others. Don't try to do something bigger just to be bigger than someone else. Be what God wants you to be. You are responsible to Him for the use of your talents and abilities not for what someone else has.

Some leaders trying to avoid the use of numbers wind up doing nothing. They have no specific goals and thus no way to evaluate their work. They never try to improve themselves or their organization. They will watch a situation deteriorate before doing anything about it. Such apathy and laziness is not a characteristic of the spiritual leader. There is always room for improvement. The Lord deserves our very best!

It has been my experience that numbers are vital to proper evaluation. Consider the Sunday School class that continues to decline in attendance over an extended period of time. An evaluation must be made. It would never be made had not the numbers been evident, showing the decline. The reason for the decline is another subject that takes careful evaluation and consideration of all the facts. Leaders who do not care what happens and do nothing to change things are only revealing that they are not worthy to be leaders.

Good leaders do have a strategy. It is essential, not optional. In one sense, we all have a strategy whether written or not, whether good or bad. The strategy of some is mediocrity. They simply do nothing but try to maintain the status quo—which is impossible.

The next chapter considers how to develop and use your strategy. If you are presently serving as a spiritual leader, why not take a break from reading, and start writing down your strategy? Don't forget to set goals in your personal life and family life, as well as your organization life.

☑ LEADER'S CHECKLIST

1. What are your objectives? List three major ones.
2. Write your own definition of an objective and a goal.
3. Do you have a philosophy of ministry? Does it include

the five things mentioned in the beginning of this chapter?

4. Do you have a strategy for your personal life? Your family life? Your organizational life? Describe these strategies in one or two paragraphs each.

5. Are you able to set realistic goals? Specific goals? Name some of your goals for the year, the month, the week.

6. Does competition or adversity cause you to set more goals and try harder to reach them? Can you think of a recent example?

17

How to Develop a Good Strategy— and Use It

THE basic purpose of a good strategy is, of course, to give glory to God in all we do (see 1 Cor. 10:31). The leader will also be committed to doing his best in everything, and influencing the greatest amount of people he possibly can for the cause of Jesus Christ.

A good strategy flows out of a life lived for the glory of God. If the leader's purpose in life is to have the largest church in the world, or become the most famous speaker of all time, etc., then his strategy will reflect these selfish motives, and not the glory of God.

What Objectives Should a Spiritual Leader Have?

A good strategy is composed of objectives, goals, priorities, planning and guidelines. Every leader will be different in designing his strategy. However, the spiritual leader will usually come up with objectives that are similar to those of other spiritual leaders. Objectives are the basic purposes of the organization.

Our church has three basic objectives that control what we do and teach: evangelism, edification and expansion. The definitions of each of those objectives is so very important. Not every one will agree on the definitions we use, but that really is not important to our discussion. The important thing is to make sure when you write out your objectives that you give clear definitions so people know exactly what your organization's purposes are. It tells you much about that organization.

In our case, *evangelism* is the proclamation of the gospel to nonbelievers, resulting in their conversion to Jesus Christ, baptism in water, and membership in the local body of believers.

Some strategies of local churches design the objective of evangelism as being the sharing of the gospel to the nonbelieving world. That is good. But, it doesn't go far enough in our opinion, and the rest of the strategy is affected. The goals of the organization are the specific ways in which the objectives will be measured and accomplished. How can you design specific goals that are measurable in the area of baptism or church membership if they are not a part of your objective? Church growth is deeply affected by this point.

A conversation with a pastor in our area convinced me of the importance of baptism and church membership as a part of the basic objective of evangelism. (I was already convinced from Acts 2:41!) He and his church were quite committed to sharing the gospel with nonbelievers, and they had experienced many conversions to Christ. In fact, if all the people they had won to Christ had become responsible members of his church, that church would be the largest on the West Coast!

As it was, it was a church of moderate size that had not grown numerically in several years. After talking with him about this, I realized the problem. They were not concerned about baptism and church membership in their view of evangelism. The strategy they had was fine in one area, but very deficient in others.

Whatever your objectives, make sure they state the basic purposes of your organization in enough detail so that people know how to design goals that can be measured and accomplished. Spiritual leaders who want to do everything to the glory of God should also make sure that the objectives are based upon the Word of God (write in the Scripture references for people to study).

How to Design Specific Goals for Your Ministry

Goals are the specific ways in which the purposes of your organization will be measured and accomplished. According to most leaders I have talked with, writing specific goals is the problem. Very few do it. Goals should be written out frequently. They can change. Objectives remain the same.

In order to design specific goals for your ministry, a few basic points should be kept in mind.

Write Personal, Family and Organizational Goals

Your personal goals might involve recreation and exercise for health reasons, reading or writing books, traveling to various parts of the world, attending special seminars and conferences, etc. These personal goals will affect your organizational goals but they are not the same. Personal goals deal with the growth of the leader himself. Organizational goals deal with the organization's growth. The leader needs to grow regardless of the organization he is involved with.

Family goals, like vacations, sports/games, house, cars, investments, financial security, etc., are often affected by the organizational goals. The matter of priorities will often determine which takes precedent over the other. The leader's family is more important than the organization, but the way that importance is emphasized or determined is not an easy matter!

Once you can see on paper the specific goals you have in each area, you are in a better position to evaluate the possibility of accomplishing these goals. You can see immediately where overlapping and conflict exist.

Set Both Immediate and Long-range Goals

Long-range goals teach patience. They help you stick to the task in the midst of temporary setbacks. They encourage a longer ministry in one job and place. They give direction to the immediate goals. Immediate goals should be designed in an effort to accomplish long-range goals. Long-range goals can be based on any length of time within a person's lifetime.

It has been my experience that long-range goals that exceed 10 years in length are normally changed. So, a long-range goal to me is one that covers a 10-year period of time. At the end of the 10 years, write out goals for the next 10 years, and so on.

Long-range goals of 10 years in length should include some five-year goals as well. This gives you a point for evaluation in achieving the 10-year goals. Evaluate the first five years on the basis of whether that experience will produce the 10-year goals. If not, then change what you are doing!

Immediate goals can be based on the day, week, month or year. Perhaps all of those should be used. I have a few specific goals in mind for each day. I like to write them down. There are immediate goals for this coming week that I must accomplish. In our ministry, our leaders must evaluate what we are doing every three months. We have what we call a quarterly planning session. We meet all day

> *It is better to achieve your goals than to be impressed with the size of them but never achieve them.*

in an isolated place. Ideas are freely shared and goals determined, changed or dropped.

Churches should establish specific goals for their ministries at least every year. The best time to do this is early summer. Plan the church year as though it begins in September.

There are four basic patterns in the ministry of every church upon which you can base your planning: the first runs from after Labor Day until Christmas; the second runs from after New Year's Day until Easter week; the third runs from after Easter week until school is out; and the fourth pattern is the summer—basically, July and August. Learn to plan and write specific goals for those four periods of time.

Try not to overlap what you are doing into another pattern. Each summer you should reevaluate your goals. Did you achieve them? What could you do differently or better?

Set Deadlines for Accomplishing Your Goals
A common fallacy in thinking is that we can work on a particular matter at another time. There is no deadline, no time limit. As a result, the matter is usually put off until

someone demands it be done by a certain time. Set deadlines for your goals. When is a project to be completed? Most leaders find that they are more productive when they have deadlines.

We publish a church newsletter. We learned that a deadline had to be set for the submission of articles for that newsletter. If the article was not submitted on time, it would have to wait for the next issue. No exceptions! It has a way of making everyone set goals and plan ahead!

As soon as the time limit for accomplishing your goals is over, immediately evaluate your goals. Do you need to establish other goals based on what you just did? Did you achieve your goals on time? Do you need to set another time limit?

Make Your Goals Realistic

Goals should relate realistically to available time, resources and personnel. Be careful about this. It is better to achieve your goals than to be impressed with the size of them but never achieve them!

People will get discouraged if they can never achieve the goals which the spiritual leadership designs. Once several goals are achieved, then the faith and vision of the people can be stretched a little more. Set goals that will encourage the people and be realistic for them to accomplish.

If it normally takes two years to build a building the size you want, then don't set a goal of six months! Use your head! Set goals realistically.

One of the goals we set for our church one summer was to visit 17,000 homes in our immediate community, introducing ourselves, our ministry as a church and our Lord Jesus Christ. We set the goal deadline. It was to be accomplished in eight weeks by people going out one night a week for about one hour of visiting. Over 200 people participated. The goal was reachable because we had spent time in evaluating the number of homes, the time in which to do it and the personnel available to do the work. It was a realistic goal for us.

Relate Goals to Objectives

Every goal should be directly related to one of the basic objectives of the organization. Setting a goal just to have a goal is not good strategy. People will get tired of that. It ought to be simple to read a goal and immediately know what objective it is related to. If the objective is not the purpose of the goal, then the goal will detract from the effectiveness of the organization. It will drain off manpower, money and time. The organization cannot stand many of these additional, beyond-the-objectives goals. They are growth-restricting obstacles whether they are recognized as such or not.

If the objective in a given organization is evangelism, but one of the goals is to take people to Israel to study archaeology, that organization will be weakened by the goal. The goal does not accomplish the objective. Leaders should learn to avoid goals that take people away from the main objectives of the organization.

Communicate Goals in Advance

Goals should be communicated well in advance of the time period planned for accomplishing them. Many mistakes are made in this area. A few leaders establish goals and then announce them to the people who are to be involved in accomplishing the goals the week before the project or task begins! It's not enough time. People need to be prepared mentally for what is expected of them.

In our church, it has been our experience that goals

affecting the entire church must be planned and communicated at least six months in advance. The two months before a certain project, task, or ministry begins is the most crucial time of communication. All parties involved must have time to prepare for the project. There must be sufficient time for promoting the project—one week a public announcement, another week a mailing, another week a sign, another week a skit, another week a brochure, etc. Goals must be continually communicated. Don't pull any surprises on your people and then complain when the response is not good and the goal is not accomplished!

How Do You Determine Priorities?

In any effective strategy, leaders must establish priorities. Priorities are the factors that determine when and why things are done. When you have a great many goals, you must decide which ones are most important for you to work on today, and in what order.

Don't Overdo It!

Sometimes a leader is trying to accomplish too many goals. That's another reason why we need to establish priorities. Some leaders who are workaholics have a tendency to design too many goals for themselves and other employees. They will drive themselves and others until someone has a breakdown! Rome wasn't built in a day, and you'll be much happier if you don't try!

One simple way to establish priorities among all the goals that people want to accomplish is by putting a value system on the goals. Have a category called "most important," then "somewhat important," then "not quite so important" and, of course, "not important at all"!

Priorities and Time

In dealing with priorities you must establish the time involved to do it. Here is where many leaders fail. Some people like to spell priority t-i-m-e! If I tell my wife that she is a priority in my life but I spend no time alone with her, she should begin to wonder about my claim!

The first thing is to set a deadline for completing a

Learn to do the "must" things first. Your mental attitude and response will be much more relaxed when facing other priorities.

---

given goal. Next, you must estimate the time needed to accomplish this goal by the desired deadline. Then, you must plan segments of time into your weekly calendar that will meet the demands of that goal. If it is not important to you (a matter of priorities), you probably won't spend time on it!

Let's try to illustrate the matter of priorities by picturing a leader working at his desk in his office. His secretary calls him on the phone and gives him this message: "Your wife is on the phone." Some leaders will immediately take the call, especially when the wife is not known to abuse the privilege, because it is a priority to them.

Suppose the secretary calls and says, "Your wife called and said to pick up your suit at the cleaners." Immediately, you must evaluate the importance of that call and the time needed to act upon it. If you don't need the suit for a few days, it would seem ridiculous to get up immediately and go to the cleaners for the suit.

Sometimes emergencies must be handled, and these have a way of demonstrating priorities. Suppose the secretary called and said, "Leave your office; the building is on fire!" It shouldn't take you too long to respond! We all need to learn the lesson of time. Priorities will determine when you do something and for how long you must do it.

The Difference Between "Must" and "Could"

In order for priorities to function properly, a leader must discern the difference between that which must be done today and that which, although extremely important, could wait until tomorrow. Learn to do the "must" things first. Your mental attitude and response will be much more relaxed when facing other priorities.

Some priorities should be fixed in given time slots each week. There are certain things that should be done at the same time every week. If one of your priorities is to spend one day a week with your wife alone, then schedule it! Whenever you have the opportunity to do something else on that day, you must ask the question, "Is it a higher priority than my wife?"

Priorities and Commitment

Priorities are built primarily upon your commitment. What you believe is important comes from what you have committed yourself to do or be. The spiritual leader must begin with his personal commitment to the Lord. That is best understood in a time of private prayer and study of the Word. If it is the priority you say it is, then schedule a time each day for it and keep your appointments!

A spiritual leader must also be committed to his wife and family. Again, schedule those times, and keep your promises! A leader must also have a commitment to other members of the Body of Christ. What time do you give to this each week? We must also be committed to the world around us. Again, what time is given for this?

Our commitment to the work of Christ must also be scheduled. If, as a spiritual leader, you work full-time as a salaried employee in the Lord's work, then the time you give is fairly well structured for you. But if you are not full-time, then you must decide how much time you can give to the Lord's work. Time often tells us what the real priorities of our life are.

The "R&R" Priority

One final thing before we leave the subject of priorities. Many leaders do not carefully evaluate the importance of time given to protect one's health. This involves diet, rest, exercise and relaxation. Leaders feel the pressure of achievement and being an example to others. Leaders do not want to have others accuse them of laziness or lack of desire to work. They often feel embarrassed about taking time off, or spending time each week in physical exercise and recreation.

Some, of course, abuse this need, spend too much time at it and thus neglect more important things. However, the facts show that the real problem among most aggressive leader-types is the failure to schedule time for rest, relaxation and recreation.

It is easy to prove the fallacy of the kind of thinking that keeps us working to achieve goals without taking time off from work. Longevity is greatly reduced, humanly speaking, when we do not have proper rest, diet and exercise. Heart attacks are frequent among leaders (often at an early age).

Leaders have a tendency or responsibility to sit at a desk during the day. They do not move around as they should.

They ride in cars when they should walk and take elevators when they should walk the stairs. We learn to enjoy the luxuries of life, and forget about our physical condition.

Many Christian organizations will do well to check up on their leaders in this particular area. More can be accomplished in 30 years than in 10, even at a slower pace! Your health is a priority to you right now. The effectiveness of leaders in their present work is affected by the kind of diet, rest and recreation that they have.

Four Essentials of Good Planning

Good strategies are based on careful planning. Planning is the process by which we seek ways to achieve our goals. Planning takes time as well as foresight. We must constantly anticipate and think ahead. That for which we plan may have no existence outside our own minds, but it is a vital part of strategy. Sometimes your plans do not materialize. When this happens, it is no time for discouragement, but rather an opportunity to see God work things out for His glory in spite of your unfulfilled plans.

Proverbs 15:22 says, "Without consultation, plans are frustrated, but with many counselors they succeed." It takes time to plan. There are many details to be worked out and problems to solve. Talking with others about it is important to the success of your plans. If you have five minutes to achieve a goal, spend two of those minutes planning.

Some leaders think that planning is the opposite of trusting God. That kind of thinking is similar to the preacher who believes that he doesn't need to study because he wants to be led of the Holy Spirit while preaching! Obviously, God can lead and direct us in our planning! We must depend upon His guidance at that point as well as in the actual ministry for which we are planning. There are four essential ingredients to good planning.

Personnel

Describing who is involved, who is responsible and who will do the work is vital to good planning. The name of the

---

Failure to plan for obstacles almost insures that they will come! Good planning must anticipate problems.

---

game here is communication. The leader starts the process in his own mind, and begins by considering which personnel are in the chain of command and responsibility. Include them first in your planning.

Next, begin to communicate with others who will be affected by the planning and include their ideas and suggestions. Determine which personnel will be responsible for what areas of the plan. Make assignments with deadlines. Make sure the personnel involved in the planning know who to report to when their work is done.

In my early ministry I thought that the fewest personnel possible should do the planning. There are still times when that must be done. But, experience has shown me that the more people involved in the planning process, the greater measure of success. Take it in stages, and decide when to include others, but seek to include as many as possible at the right times. This often takes the wisdom of Solomon!

Resources

The most important resource we have is the ministry of the Holy Spirit in the lives of people. These are not the personnel who do the planning, but the people who will carry out the project—those who actually do the work. Materials can be replaced or discarded, but people cannot. God works through people!

In addition to the people, you must evaluate in your planning what materials will be needed to carry out the project or goal. Will it be a brochure or a letter? Will it be a sign or sound equipment? Will it be tables and chairs or a room to rent? These and many more questions like them will have to be pursued.

There is also the matter of finances. Very few projects can be accomplished without the expenditure of money. Good planning pays much attention to cost. Leaders who do not evaluate such matters will soon lose the support of those around them. It is easy in most cases to determine how much a project will cost. The problem comes when deciding how to raise the money that will be needed. Where the money comes from is a vital question to good planning.

Obstacles

Failure to plan for obstacles almost insures that they will come! Good planning must anticipate problems that can develop. It must also discuss how to overcome obstacles, whether they be financial or merely the opinions of people. Overcoming obstacles is not what every person likes to do, but it is necessary and it seems to be a quality of leadership.

The late Dr. Bob Jones, Sr., had a saying like this: "The test of your character is what it takes to stop you!" How true that is! Many give up too easily. The obstacles, problems or difficulties seem too great to overcome so the project is abandoned. But wait a minute! Was it a worthwhile goal? Will it meet a real need? Will it give glory to God? Is it based on biblical authority? Is it the will of God? Obstacles are there as tests to our faith, as well as sometimes indicating a closed door.

When anyone says, "It can't be done," it makes men of faith hurt inside. They feel that God has been questioned. Jesus said, "With men it is impossible, but not with God; for all things are possible with God" (Mark 10:27). When facing obstacles, it is good to look at the alternatives you have.

1. The door is closed; go no farther in pursuing your goal.
2. We have overlooked something that is being brought to our attention by the obstacle we face.
3. Our faith needs to be tested.
4. The obstacle will increase our dedication and commitment.
5. There is another way of doing it.
6. We are being reminded of our limitations; it causes us to depend more upon God.

Don't be afraid of obstacles. They can turn out to be great blessings in disguise! Learn to plan for them and prepare to face them.

Evaluation

The failure to evaluate goals both before and after they are achieved is a serious mistake. No planning can be really effective that does not take evaluation seriously. The best time to evaluate is immediately after a goal is achieved or when it has failed. Ask many questions with the word "why" in them. For example:

1. Why did so few young people attend that occasion?
2. Why did we fail to communicate to our adults?
3. Why did the expense exceed the budget we set?
4. Why did the people feel we had not considered their needs and feelings in the matter?
5. Why was the sound equipment not effective?

Put your evaluation on paper and file it in a place to which you will turn often for help and advice. If some particular idea failed miserably, then write down the reasons why and file it for future protection. After all, you don't want to make the same mistake twice.

In all this discussion concerning planning, remember that it also takes time. Is there time in your schedule for planning? If not, why not? Could it be because there are no specific goals governing your life? Leaders really have no choice—they must plan, or they had better plan to fail.

The most important planning time for the leader is the time he spends alone. Do not begin to plan with others until you have had time to plan and think on the project or goals involved. You must be mentally prepared when taking time to plan with others.

Why Do We Need Guidelines?

Without guidelines our plans will often fail or, at best, lose their ring of authority and urgency. Guidelines should be established that will cover different situations and various kinds of goals. They must allow for flexibility and change, but they must also be enforced and applied. If you cannot enforce your guidelines, you might have the wrong set of guidelines or you yourself may be lacking in good leadership.

The subject of guidelines is very much related to a previous chapter on authority. Morality is in the background. Without a standard of morality it is almost impossible to establish guidelines. The spiritual leader bases his guidelines upon the morality of the Scriptures.

Guidelines are the moral and ethical framework in which the organization will seek to accomplish its goals. Without them, the organization loses the perspective of its original objectives and often uses methods that cause the eventual decline of that organization. Guidelines keep us on the right track and faithful to our original commitments.

Here are a few guidelines that illustrate what they are and how they affect the Christian organization:

Nothing shall be done which violates a principle of God's Word. In our staff meetings, a discussion which brings up a matter that is in violation of God's Word immediately ends. We cannot do it.

Emphasis shall be upon people rather than upon tasks to be done. One of our objectives in our church is edification, which involves the building up of people to maturity in Christ. It is more important to build the person, than to use the person to build the work.

All ministries and activities should be evaluated in the light of our objectives. This is simply a reminder to all of us to stick to the objectives. It is relatively easy to develop goals that have nothing to do with our objectives.

Methods of training shall concentrate on the discipleship of the few to reach the many, and this to be done by mature believers. Our experience has proven the importance of this guideline. Using immature people in leadership roles hinders the accomplishment of our objectives.

Trying to motivate the masses of people is not nearly as successful as motivating the few to reach the many.

All positions of leadership and service are to be based upon a godly life-style. Enough said. Breakdowns in strategies are often found at this point!

Gifts, abilities, or talents will be confirmed by others in this body of believers before a person is placed into leadership. We all think better of ourselves than we actually are. We need the evaluations of other people before we place people into leadership.

The list of guidelines could be expanded. It simply reveals the moral and ethical framework in which we seek to accomplish our goals. The guidelines are vital to the matter of spiritual commitment.

Again: a good strategy is composed of five elements:

- *Objectives*—the basic purposes of the organization.
- *Goals*—the specific ways in which the purposes of the organization will be measured and accomplished.
- *Priorities*—the factors that determine when and why things are done.
- *Planning*—the process used to achieve the goals (includes personnel, resources, obstacles and evaluation).
- *Guidelines*—the moral and ethical framework in which the organization will seek to accomplish its goals.

☑ Leader's Checklist

1. What are your organization's objectives? Do you have a clear definition for each of these?
2. How frequently do you write out your goals for your personal life? Family life? Organizational life?

3. Do you have immediate as well as long-range goals?
4. Have you prioritized your goals?
5. Does your planning include the "four essentials"?
6. Do you have guidelines for establishing your objectives? Are they written down?

18

A STRATEGY FOR GROWTH

A strategy is important for any organization. Leaders understand the reasons why it is needed and what happens when a clear strategy has not been developed. Some organizations base their strategy on loyalty to their purposes and objectives. While commendable and right, it does not necessarily include growth. Many organizations simply maintain the status quo and are content with it. There is no planning and projecting of future growth.

Churches and missionary organizations have traditionally been slow to include growth as a part of strategy. To some believers, it smacks of carnality and "Madison Avenue" marketing and approaches. We often view "growth talk" as carnal and immature.

WHAT DO WE MEAN BY GROWTH?

A strategy of growth has to evaluate the meaning of growth and decide what kinds of growth are to be included in the planning and implementation of that strategy. Growth suggests increase and productivity; that usually involves numbers.

The basic factor of church growth is the sovereignty of God. First Corinthians 3:6-8 makes this point:

> I planted, Apollos watered, but God was causing the growth. So then neither the one who plants nor the one who waters is anything, but God who causes the growth. Now he who plants and he who waters are one; but each will receive his own reward according to his own labor.

Numerical Growth

God causes the growth. The evaluation and analysis of what God does or can do puts us in the problem of "numbers." In some strategies, an increase in attendance over the previous year in the public church services is all that is meant by growth.

Reports and statistics of increases in attendance on a week-by-week basis are absent in the New Testament account of church life and growth. But numbers are there, and a good strategy that is based on biblical teaching will consider numerical growth as a part of that strategy.

Acts 2:41 speaks of growth when the church began, and reports: "So then, those who had received his word were baptized; and there were added that day about three thousand souls." Verse 47 continues: "And the Lord was adding to their number day by day those who were being saved."

Acts 5:14 uses the word "added" again: "And all the more believers in the Lord, multitudes of men and women, were constantly added to their number." Acts 11:24 contains the fourth and final usage of the word "added" in Acts, and translates it as "brought": "For he was a good man, and full of the Holy Spirit and of faith. And considerable numbers were brought to the Lord." Obviously, numbers are important in the work of the Lord.

In addition to the word "added" we read in Acts 6:1: "Now at this time while the disciples were increasing in number." Acts 9:31 says: "So the church throughout all Judea and Galilee and Samaria enjoyed peace, being built

---

The evidence is clear—numbers are important in evaluating growth and in developing a strategy of growth.

---

up; and, going on in the fear of the Lord and in the comfort of the Holy Spirit, it continued to increase."

In Acts 16:5, this report was given concerning Paul and Silas returning to the churches of Paul's first missionary journey where he and Barnabas had originally labored: "So the churches were being strengthened in the faith, and were increasing in number daily."

While the statement could refer to a daily increase in the number of churches, it seems more likely, on the basis of Acts 15:41, that this phrase, "increasing in number daily," was referring to the growth of the churches already established.

Numbers Reported in the New Testament

The evidence is clear—numbers are important in evaluating growth and in developing a strategy of growth. While attendance averages are not reported, the number of converts being added to the church is. If our evaluation of the

New Testament record is correct, the following things were a part of the growth and the numerical record of it:

1. Decisions to become Christians.
2. Baptisms to proclaim faith publicly.
3. Additions to church membership.

In a strategy of growth, all three categories should be a vital part of planning and reporting. While actual attendance figures are often a barometer indicating the growth of a local church, they are not the heart of what concerns the biblical record. Attendance can be affected by facilities and parking. Attendance can also be a difficult evaluation to make. With multiple services and ministries, people are reached and become involved through many channels which may or may not be reflected in the public service attendance records of the church.

WHAT IS SPIRITUAL GROWTH?

Spiritual growth is hard to measure. Second Peter 3:18 urges believers to grow in the grace and knowledge of our Lord Jesus Christ, but how do we evaluate that growth?

Elements of Spiritual Growth
One of the best passages on spiritual growth is found in Colossians 1:9-12:

> For this reason also, since the day we heard of it, we have not ceased to pray for you and to ask that you may be filled with the knowledge of His will in all spiritual wisdom and understanding, so that you may walk in a manner worthy of the Lord, to please Him in all respects, bearing fruit in every

good work and increasing in the knowledge of God; strengthened with all power, according to His glorious might, for the attaining of all steadfastness and patience; joyously giving thanks to the Father, who has qualified us to share in the inheritance of the saints in light.

In this passage, the following phrases refer to spiritual growth:

- "filled with the knowledge of His will"
- "walk in a manner worthy of the Lord"
- "to please Him in all respects"
- "bearing fruit in every good work"
- "increasing in the knowledge of God"
- "strengthened with all power"
- "steadfastness and patience"
- "joyously giving thanks."

First Peter 2:2-3 puts it this way: "Like newborn babes, long for the pure milk of the word, that by it you may grow in respect to salvation, if you have tasted the kindness of the Lord." This is not instruction for new converts, but for all believers who desire to grow spiritually. We are to desire God's Word "like newborn babes" desire the milk of their mothers' breasts. The reference is to an intense desire, not a casual concern.

Gifts and Spiritual Growth for the Body
Ephesians 4:11-16 is one of the finest passages on the spiritual growth of the Church. It begins with a listing of gifted leaders, and ends with the interrelationship of all the members one with another:

> And He gave some as apostles, and some as prophets, and some as evangelists, and some as pastors and teachers, for the equipping of the saints for the work of service, to the building up of the body of Christ; until we all attain to the unity of the faith, and of the knowledge of the Son of God, to a mature man, to the measure of the stature which belongs to the fulness of Christ. As a result, we are no longer to be children, tossed here and there by waves, and carried about by every wind of doctrine, by the trickery of men, by craftiness in deceitful scheming; but speaking the truth in love, we are to grow up in all aspects into Him, who is the head, even Christ, from whom the whole body, being fitted and held together by that which every joint supplies, according to the proper working of each individual part, causes the growth of the body for the building up of itself in love.

One of the interesting points about growth in this passage is that it refers to the growth of the *Body*, not simply the individual. Individual spiritual growth is, of course, essential, but this passage focuses on the spiritual growth of the entire church as members use their spiritual gifts to encourage and edify one another.

Using their spiritual gifts and equipped with biblical preaching and teaching, the believers will build each other up and spiritual growth will occur.

This process involves three things:

1. *Doctrinal unity*—"the unity of the faith, and of the knowledge of the Son of God."
2. *Personal integrity*—"speaking the truth (literally, 'truthing') in love."

3. *Corporate harmony*—"being fitted and held together."

The result of these three things is edification or spiritual growth.

The Word and the Work

The gifted leaders (apostles, prophets, evangelists and pastor/teachers) do the equipping of the believers. Paul reveals that the equipping process is achieved by the preaching and teaching of God's Word:

> All Scripture is inspired by God and profitable for teaching, for reproof, for correction, for training in righteousness; that the man of God may be adequate, equipped for every good work (2 Tim. 3:16-17).

The Scriptures will equip us for "every good work." That is the work of the gifted leaders. The believers who are thus equipped are involved in "the work of service" (ministry). Too often churches are hindered in the growth process due to the fact that the gifted leaders are the ones who do the work of ministering, while the majority in the congregation sit in the pews and watch!

The "work of service" is referred to in 1 Peter 4:10-11, and indicates the exercise of spiritual gifts:

> As each one has received a special gift, employ it in serving one another, as good stewards of the manifold grace of God. Whoever speaks, let him speak, as it were, the utterances of God; whoever serves, let him do so as by the strength which God supplies; so that in all things God may be glorified

through Jesus Christ, to whom belongs the glory
and dominion forever and ever. Amen.

The arena in which all true spiritual growth occurs is
love. First Corinthians 8:1 reminds us that knowledge only
produces pride; it is love that edifies.

A strategy of growth must include more than the
numerical increases in decisions, baptisms and membership. It must also include planning and preparation for
the spiritual growth of the church. The strategy must focus
on biblical priorities. It must be careful not to confuse roles
and responsibilities between the gifted leaders and the
members of the Body.

STRATEGY AND THE GREAT COMMISSION

No strategy of growth could possibly be complete without
including the task laid upon the church by our Lord Jesus
Christ. Without it, our strategy is nearsighted. The so-called
"Great Commission" is found in the following passages:

> **Matthew 28:19-20:** Go therefore and make disci-
> ples of all the nations, baptizing them in the name
> of the Father and the Son and the Holy Spirit,
> teaching them to observe all that I commanded
> you; and lo, I am with you always, even to the end
> of the age.

> **Mark 16:15-16:** Go into all the world and preach
> the gospel to all creation. He who has believed and
> has been baptized shall be saved; but he who has
> disbelieved shall be condemned.

> **Luke 24:47-49:** And that repentance for forgive-

ness of sins should be proclaimed in His name to all the nations, beginning from Jerusalem. You are witnesses of these things. And behold, I am sending forth the promise of My Father upon you; but you are to stay in the city until you are clothed with power from on high.

John 20:21: Peace be with you; as the Father has sent Me, I also send you.

Acts 1:8: But you shall receive power when the Holy Spirit has come upon you; and you shall be My witnesses both in Jerusalem, and in all Judea and Samaria, and even to the remotest part of the earth.

The Task and the Power

If we understand Christ's instructions, they were primarily given to the apostles whom He sent out around the world with His message. They, along with others, were eye-witnesses. In a secondary sense, we are also His witnesses, those who believe in the message of the Bible and have personally experienced the wonderful salvation and spiritual birth that is promised through our trust in the death of Jesus Christ for our sins, and His resurrection from the dead!

The Great Commission becomes the task of all churches. Every strategy of growth must be deeply concerned with it. It includes the following:

1. *Authority*—"as the Father has sent Me, I also send you."
2. *Ability*—"clothed with power from on high" and

"you shall receive power when the Holy Spirit has come upon you."
3. *Aim*—"make disciples of all the nations."
4. *Action*—"Go into all the world."
5. *Approach*—"preach the gospel" and "you shall be My witnesses."
6. *Area*—"all the nations," "all the world" and "the remotest part of the earth."
7. *Assurance*—"and lo, I am with you always, even to the end of the age."

God is the one who saves and causes the growth. He uses the believer who is willing to go. The task does not center on "come" but on "go." The field is the world, and the opportunities are tremendous. God "opens" and "shuts" the doors of opportunity (1 Cor. 16:9; Col. 4:3).

Penetrating Cultures

Our strategy of growth in reaching the many cultures, countries and cities of this world requires trained workers who are ready to minister in cross-cultural and cross-linguistic ethnic groups. Our strategy leaves no one out—we are to disciple "all the nations" (Gentile ethnic groups).

It certainly must include the different languages spoken throughout the world, many of whom have yet to receive one verse of Scripture in their own tongue. We must involve ourselves greatly in the selection and training of workers to reach cross-cultural and cross-linguistic groups, working with agencies and organizations who are better skilled than we are to understand the needs of our changing world.

Paul presents the challenge:

For "Whoever will call upon the name of the Lord

will be saved." How then shall they call upon Him in whom they have not believed? And how shall they believe in Him whom they have not heard? And how shall they hear without a preacher? And how shall they preach unless they are sent? Just as it is written, "How beautiful are the feet of those who bring glad tidings of good things!" (Rom. 10:13-15).

We need more "beautiful feet" in our strategy of growth and in our desire to reach our world for Jesus Christ!

Elements of Our Strategy

Selecting and supporting workers. The selection, sending and support of the workers are crucial elements in fulfilling the Great Commission. The opportunities abound, but the workers are few.

What shall be our strategy for increasing the number of workers? Jesus gave us the answer:

> And seeing the multitudes, He felt compassion for them, because they were distressed and downcast like sheep without a shepherd. Then He said to His disciples, "The harvest is plentiful, but the workers are few. Therefore beseech the Lord of the harvest to send out workers into His harvest" (Matt. 9:36-38).

Our strategy must include prayer! Much talk about the need of workers may be helpful at times; at other times, it may be keeping us from doing what ought to be done—prayer for the Lord to send out the workers.

Prayer, workers, etc., are crucial, but so is the support of the workers. A proper strategy of growth concerns itself with this vital element. How will the work be financed? How much money will be needed?

First Corinthians 9:14 says the Lord directed that the ones who take the gospel to others should be supported in their efforts. The laborer is worthy of his hire. It is the responsibility of the churches to support the workers who go with the gospel message into the world and seek to establish God's church in every country, culture, and city. With rising costs around the world, the responsibility is great upon the sending church. We need a greater vision and a greater commitment to reach our lost world for Jesus Christ.

Growing disciples. An effective strategy of growth will be directed at the result of making disciples in a world that desperately needs to hear the gospel of Jesus Christ. It will include the following kinds of growth:

1. *Numerical growth* through the proclamation of the gospel resulting in decisions for Christ, baptisms and responsible church membership.
2. *Spiritual growth* through gifted leaders equipping the church with biblical preaching and teaching, members using their spiritual gifts, building up one another in the sphere of God's love.
3. *Extension growth* through the sending and supporting of workers into cross-cultural and cross-linguistic areas of the world to plant God's church in every ethnic grouping.

Planting New Churches

Extension growth occurs within our own culture as well. The planting of churches in every community remains a goal of the Church of Jesus Christ. That community may be dominated by another culture and language group within our own nation, or it may represent people with the same cultural background and life-styles as our own. The goal remains unchanged—planting God's church, making disciples of all the nations!

It has been my privilege to be involved personally in the planting of a church. From the beginning, there were doubt, questions, confusion, anxiety and struggles. But God was faithful. As people came to know the Lord, were baptized and became responsible members of the church, the church grew. From that church, others churches were born, and missionaries were sent around the world.

After the joys of planting a church and watching its leadership develop and grow, it was my pleasure to once again be involved in church development, growth, and plantings. I became the pastor of the church where I grew up. In over 14 years of ministry we saw the church grow through evangelism, making of disciples and equipping the members.

The mother church began to plant other churches, and we had the joy of seeing many workers leave that church to begin to plant other churches in many parts of the world. Not only were churches planted in other communities with our same cultural background, we saw churches planted whose ministry was conducted in other languages.

Church planting around the world continues to be the primary strategy. After many years of ministry in a growing church in Orange County, California, we have seen the planting of a cross-linguistic and cross-cultural church, as well as the establishment of another church within our own culture, but miles removed from our immediate communities.

We have workers around the world planting God's

church on other continents and in far-away places unknown to most of us. But, the joy is there and the privilege is great. Our strategy of growth continues to affect our ministry and keep our eyes on our Savior's desire that we make disciples of all the nations.

One of the greatest needs in the lives of spiritual leaders in God's churches is to develop a strategy of growth that keeps our eyes upon the world. When we see only our own problems and struggles and we do not look beyond our borders at the "multitudes," we not only miss out on the great opportunity of our Lord's commission to us, we will find that this lack of vision and commitment will begin to affect us in our local situations.

People need to see the world as the Lord sees it. He was moved with compassion when He saw the condition of people—sheep without a shepherd, lost and needing to be found. In Luke 15, three parables (the lost sheep, lost coin, and lost son) reveal the heart of our Lord. Luke 19:10 tells us that the Son of Man came to seek and to save that which is lost.

May God put on our hearts what is on His heart! May God open the eyes of our local church leaders and cause them to see other cultures, languages and people groups in need of the gospel and the planting of churches.

☑ LEADER'S CHECKLIST

1. What do you believe about numerical growth?
2. What statistics should be kept in the strategy for church growth?
3. What do you believe is spiritual growth? How do you measure it? How do you know if it is happening?

4. What essentials do you see that we need in developing a strategy of growth for the local church?
5. How do we get more workers for the nations of the world?
6. What do you believe about the Great Commission? How can we include it in our strategy of growth?
7. Why do many local churches lack a vision for the world?
8. What can spiritual leaders do to encourage a strategy of growth in the local church? What do you plan to do?

LAW VII

LOVE:
You Need to Care for the People Around You

19

IT'S NOT EASY TO LOVE PEOPLE!

THE badge of discipleship is love for one another (see John 13:34,35). It is impossible to deal with spiritual leadership and not talk about loving people. Management books from the secular world may leave it out of the discussion, but Christians cannot.

Loving people is not as simple as it sounds! Leaders know that, but they don't often know why. Some of us give up too easily in the attempt to show love. One of our staff members has a discipleship group that meets early in the morning before the men go off to work. One day, one of the members of that group failed to show up for the Bible study. The others members decided to go to his house, wake him up, and have the Bible study right there! They didn't want him to miss out, and they loved him enough to do something about it. I don't think he'll miss one of the meetings again.

CAN LEADERS "BE WITH" THOSE WHO ARE LED?

In the secular world, leaders are sometimes separated from those working under them. Different privileges and facilities are given to the leaders, separating them from the workers. Close friendships are not cultivated between leaders and workers. They are considered to be dangerous. Leaders stay aloof from the workers. All of this reveals a failure to understand the importance of love between leader and worker.

There are certain burdens and responsibilities that only the leader can bear. He cannot share some things with the

> *There must be some time when the leader shows the ones he works with that they are more important to him than the tasks that need to be done.*

workers even though he might want to do so. But staying completely away from the people under him is a great mistake. It is a dangerous principle to isolate yourself from those with whom you work.

When Jesus called His disciples according to Mark 3:14, it was "that they might be *with Him*." Close association between the leader and the ones under that leadership is vital to effective spiritual leadership. There must be a sense of unity, fellowship, partnership and, most of all, love. Those under a spiritual leadership must know that the leader loves them and works for them.

But, let's face it, it's not easy to love certain people! God, of course, knows that problem in our lives and has provided resources for us to draw upon that will give us a love for people regardless of how unlovable they might be. Loving people does not mean being dishonest or deceitful. The arena of God's love is very practical and open for all to examine. It's a combination of little things that we do for people.

When God's love is controlling, you don't have to fake it or put on a false front. You can be real, honest and transparent before others. You can relax and enjoy your relationships with people and not be worrying about what others think of you.

For leaders, this is a special problem because they are very much aware of what others think and say of them. They are always out front for everyone to see and evaluate. Their lives are more exposed to others than most people ever experience. They must work with all types of personalities, and they do not enjoy the luxury of nonleaders who can easily walk away from a relationship because they have no responsibility.

LEADERSHIP PROBLEMS IN LOVING PEOPLE

Before we take an in-depth look at God's love, which leaders must understand and apply in their relationships with people, we need to identify the common problems which leaders have in showing love for people. Leaders will identify easily with these problems, and all prospective leaders must learn to recognize them and know how to deal with them.

Some Leaders Are Too Busy

A leader or administrator is by nature more goal-oriented than most people. The leader seeks to accomplish things and achieve as much as possible. Frequently, this causes the leader to appear, and maybe become, insensitive to people. Often the leader feels pressured by the multitude of his responsibilities and simply does not have time to spend with people with whom he works. It often becomes a matter of priorities.

To the leader, the task to be achieved seems more important than any one individual's needs or problems. There is a sense in which that is true. But it is also dangerous when people are ignored or neglected. Jesus had time for people, the individual as well as the crowd. Leaders must arrange their priorities so that time spent with people is not looked upon as time wasted or time that is not important.

It is possible to be too available to people and thus hinder the effectiveness of your leadership and the needs of others who depend upon the leader fulfilling his or her responsibilities. However, there must be some time when the leader shows the ones he works with that they are more important to him than the tasks or the projects that need to be done. If this is not done, the leader will discover that the very leadership he needs in order to accomplish those important tasks has diminished and is not there when he needs it. Love and loyalty are very closely related. The more love demonstrated between the leader and the people he leads, the stronger the ties and loyalties.

Putting Too Many Demands on Ourselves
The worst problem the leader has is himself. The leader is often more of a perfectionist than the average person. He expects things to be done right and with a certain class that speaks well of the organization or of the work he is doing. He pressures and drives himself in areas that others could handle. It is more difficult to let go than it is to take on more work. He thrives on work and normally enjoys it.

The problem that develops is rarely recognized by the leader at the time it is happening. The demands and pressures he puts upon his own life and schedule make it virtually impossible for him to have time for loving people. He justifies this by reasoning that people will appreciate the hours of hard work that he engages in, and will readily see his true motives are good and beneficial in the long run for all concerned.

However, people need love and they need to know that the leader loves them. And, frankly, that takes time! A worker may need the love and encouragement of the leader, but because of the pressure and demands upon the leader, which the leader often places upon himself, that person feels guilty for taking the valuable time of the leader.

The leader must be more relaxed and allow time for others. In a sense, he or she must become more disciplined in the use of time. Leaders must learn to allow time for showing love to others as surely as programming time for other things.

Leaders must also learn to relax more and to ease the pressure a little. They'll probably live longer if they do! Look over your schedule and responsibilities. Are there things that others could do that you are presently doing? What things could you eliminate that you do now if you were required to do so? What causes you the most pressure and frustration? How important is it that you continue doing what you are currently doing? These questions and many more must be continually asked by the leader.

The Problem of Impatience

Leaders are often impatient with those they work with, for many different reasons. Regardless of the reasons, impatience does not belong in the life-style of the spiritual leader. It is the opposite of a Spirit-filled life. People around such a leader see him or her as unloving and uncaring.

Impatience is reflected in the way we talk or look. There

are the extremes of those who talk louder or more rapidly because they are impatient or continually look at (or tap) their watches while someone is talking to them. More subtle manifestations of impatience are seen when the leader fails to delegate responsibility to others, or does something that someone under him was supposed to do but hasn't.

> *Be careful about being too sensitive. In some things our skin must be as tough as the hippopotamus.*

Sometimes what appears to be impatience to some is wisdom and good leadership to others. When someone sits in your office and continually wastes time with idle and meaningless chatter, manifesting laziness and an undisciplined life, it is not impatience to cut off such practices and force the person to go back to work. That is a part of good leadership! Leaders need wisdom at times to know the difference between impatience on their part, and good, disciplined leadership.

Impatience often develops over the speed at which others do their work. It is important that leaders do not make demands upon people that are greater than their capabilities. Sometimes a leader will expect the person under him to perform at a rate or level which the leader alone can do. This will, of course, reflect a lack of love on the part of the leader.

At times it may be a problem of discipline. Some people are lazy and procrastinate. If the leader is loving, he will take into consideration the abilities and talents of those under him, and seek to challenge without overwhelming the person. The leader will give enough time for that person to complete the task assigned, without the pressure that the leader would place upon himself but which others cannot stand. A loving leader will do all he can to protect those under him from failing. He will be patient with them and find joy in watching them grow and overcome what may have been a weakness in the past.

Insecurity About Our Position

Many leaders feel threatened. Sometimes they are threatened by bright and promising people within the organization who appear to have talents and abilities that the leader does not possess. Sometimes their insecurity comes from a lack of appreciation or acceptance. If people do not give some positive feedback to the leader from time to time, he will have a tendency to doubt and question his effectiveness and, as a result, feel threatened.

Leaders have problems with job security. This is a special problem among pastoral leaders. The average church cannot claim long pastorates in its history. Often it seems like musical chairs are being played as pastors frequently change churches in order to get a fresh start or to run away from a previous problem. A lack of success in one church can hinder a man's future in another.

Whatever the causes behind the insecurity a leader might feel, the result of this is usually a lack of love toward others. People who are insecure in their personalities, abilities or occupation have a tendency to cover up in public and hide behind past achievements. A close relationship with another person in the organization may appear to be a dangerous thing. The leader may fear what that person will do one day with what has been shared in intimate friendship. God's love is, of course, much different! But leaders are aware that human standards of love and human weaknesses can often get in the way of God's love. The results can be very threatening to the leader!

One of the most obvious symptoms of an insecure leader is a judgmental attitude toward others, especially those who represent spiritual leadership. A critical spirit flows from such a leader and derogatory remarks are common. The leader tries by criticism to strengthen his own position of authority in the eyes of others. It usually backfires!

Being Oversensitive About What Others Think
It is easy to ignore a loving response to another person on the basis of what others might think. Some pastors feel that to share a word of encouragement to one member and not to all the members is wrong. It might lead the others to think that the pastor doesn't really care about them or that he favors one member above the others.

The real issue, however, is not what others think, but what does God want us to do? Is there a real need for an encouraging word? To have a group-consciousness where you only express love in public meetings and ignore the personal times when you should be "individual-conscious" is a great mistake. The result of such action will be a leader who seems hypocritical—loving in public but not in private! People must know that a pastor is loving and kind when is is out of the pulpit as well as when he is preaching. The pastor's relationship to individuals during the week is what enhances his pulpit ministry on Sunday.

Spiritual leaders must be careful about evaluating their actions in the light of what others will think or say. The One to whom we are accountable is God Himself. When we are right with Him, it matters not what others think! That moment of sharing the love of Christ with another person will become the strength of your ministry. There will always be people who will criticize you. Be careful about being too sensitive. In some things our skin must be as tough as the hippopotamus!

The Fear of Close Relationships

Some leaders believe that close relationships and leadership are incompatible. This is unfortunate. It leads to a leadership without love, which in the final analysis is not spiritual leadership.

Leaders often build around themselves certain walls of protection that do not allow other individuals to get close to them. They fear that close relationships with others will expose them for what they are. Their faults and weaknesses become evident to the other person, and some leaders feel that when that happens they lose a certain prestige or respect in the eyes of others. You never know what that person might do with what he knows.

There is also a tendency to believe that people will not like you as much once they learn about your faults. But, Proverbs 17:17 reminds us that "A friend loves at all times, and a brother is born for adversity." In verse 9 of that same chapter it says, "He who covers a transgression seeks love, but he who repeats a matter separates intimate friends." Every leader needs that close friendship, someone who knows what he is like and still loves him and protects him.

The close friend is also the one to rebuke the leader. Proverbs 27:6 says, "Faithful are the wounds of a friend, but deceitful are the kisses of an enemy." A close friend will help the leader to have a proper perspective about situations and a clearer understanding about his own motives. Proverbs 27:17 speaks to this when it says, "Iron sharpens iron, so one man sharpens another."

Most people will never have many close friends. They may have many acquaintances and social friendships, but the circle of intimate or close friends is usually very small. That kind of friendship is developed over a long period of time and tested in many different situations. It is dangerous to share too many personal things with people who are not close friends. It takes time to build such a friendship and to have a mutual trust and love that protects and defends.

It is in the area of close friendship that a leader learns to love. When a leader isolates himself from others to the extent that he or she has no close friends, the leader's ability to grow in love is greatly reduced.

LEARNING TO LOVE PEOPLE

Learning to love people is essential to spiritual leadership. In order to overcome some of the leadership problems just mentioned, a few basic principles will be needed.

Consistency

Learn to show love to everyone and at all times. A loving leader can be counted on in times of difficulty and trial. His love is always there.

A dear friend was trying to cut down a huge tree in his front yard. A tremendous storm was in progress which was uprooting many trees. He needed help. He called me, told me his predicament and emphasized the urgency of it. I immediately rushed over to his house and helped him. It was a good thing; that tree almost crashed into the house! We were soaking wet and he turned to me and said, "Thanks, friend!" That was worth it all!

Need

If leaders are showing love, they are inevitably attracted by the needs of others. They're willing to help. First John 3:17 says, "But whoever has the world's goods, and beholds his brother in need and closes his heart against him, how does the love of God abide in him?"

One of our staff members is of great encouragement to me. Whenever I have a need, he's there. I know he loves me. I needed a car and, without another thought, he gave me his to drive as long as I wanted. He responds to needs.

Trust

A leader can destroy his effectiveness if he cannot be trusted. Can the reputation of another co-worker be placed safely in your hands when that person is absent? More friendships are destroyed through gossip than possibly anything else. Proverbs 11:13 says, "He who goes about as a talebearer reveals secrets, but he who is trustworthy conceals a matter."

Leaders must never betray confidences. Things that are shared with you in private should stay that way—private!

In a staff meeting we were discussing a certain person as to whether he would make a good leader in a certain area of ministry. The one thing against him was that he could not be trusted. He had a problem with gossip. He could not keep confidences. We decided not to place him into leadership at that time.

Self-control

Because it's not so easy to love certain people, we sometimes lose control. Leaders who fly off the handle or are always blowing off about things are demonstrating a lack of love for those around them. Self-control is a fruit of the Holy Spirit (see Gal. 5:22,23), and is a must in the life of the spiritual leader. The contrast between a person who has little except love, and a person who has much but doesn't love, is graphically illustrated in Proverbs 15:16-18.

A situation without love, according to that passage, is one where there is anger and strife.

People who work with leaders who lack self-control come to believe that they do not love them. It's a rather obvious conclusion.

Sincerity

This is the opposite of being hypocritical—a word used in ancient times for an actor who played another role by simply putting on a mask. We get our word "hypocrite" from this idea of putting on a mask. One who is sincere refuses to play the other role. He is unhypocritical. Love must be sincere and from the heart. You cannot fake it!

Many leadership problems could be resolved if leaders loved with sincerity and truth. Deception and dishonesty will destroy spiritual leadership. They will undermine people's confidence in you, and cause them to question the level of your commitment and love.

Forgiveness

Ephesians 4:32 tells us to be kind to one another, *forgiving* each other. First Peter 4:8 says that fervent love will cover a multitude of sins. Without forgiveness, leaders cannot show love. People respond to those who are forgiving and seeking to restore and rebuild relationships rather than tearing them down.

If leaders cannot forgive others for what they have said or done, the people around them will sense this bitter, unforgiving spirit, and will withdraw from close identification and support of that leader.

One lady shared with me why she was not supportive of a certain staff member. She observed his lack of forgiveness toward another lady, and did not want to experience the same kind of thing. She withdrew from that staff member's area of ministry because of it. I encouraged her to be forgiving, but I also went to the staff member and shared the importance of his forgiving the other lady. He responded well, and both ladies are now part of his ministry!

Leaders have problems loving people just like everyone else. It is easy to forget the value of love in human relationships. Song of Solomon 8:6,7 tells us that love is as strong as death, and that many waters cannot quench it, nor rivers overflow it. All the talents and abilities in the world cannot substitute for love. Leaders must put the emphasis upon it that God does. Love alone can withstand all the pressures of life and endure all the problems of people.

☑LEADER'S CHECKLIST

1. Do you find some people in your work or ministry who are hard to love? Who are they? How are you handling them?
2. Do you feel that you are "too busy" to show love to people around you?
3. If you have too many demands upon you, are there things others could do that you are presently doing to relieve you of some of the burdens? List some of those.
4. Are you patient with co-workers and others with whom you associate? Do you know what causes your impatience?
5. Can you name some symptoms of insecurity in your own life?
6. Have there been times when you were overly sensitive to what someone said? How did you overcome this?

7. Do you take time to build close relationships with other people? How?
8. Of the six basic principles of learning to love other people, which ones do you need to work on in your life?

20

HOW TO LOVE PEOPLE WITH GOD'S LOVE

THE real answer to a leader's need to love people is for him to know and experience God's love. "God is love" says 1 John 4:8. Love comes from Him. His love is very special and transcends all other kinds of love. It's different from sentimentalism and emotionalism. God's love is around when the other kinds of love run out of gas! It stays with a person in time of crisis and trouble. It's long-lasting and deeply satisfying.

The ancient Greeks knew about different kinds of love. They used at least four different words to describe love. One word expressed physical affection (*eros*). In a bad sense it referred to sexual immorality. We all understand that "making love" is not always motivated by God's love!

Another word the Greeks used (*storge*) referred to family love, the love of parents for children. It was used of the love among animals. They had another word (*phile*) to express close friendship and companionship. Jesus called His disciples "friends" in John 15:14,15 and the word is *philoi*.

The most important word for believers is the word *agape*, divine love. When the Bible speaks about God's love that we all need for one another, most of the time it uses agape. It's the love that sent Jesus Christ to the cross to die for our sins. Agape refers to acts that are unselfish. It is a giving love. It is a concern for the well-being of another person without thought of personal gain. Self-sacrifice is a fundamental idea in the word agape. It is a love that does not demand conditions before it is exercised. It is forgiving. It builds up rather than tears down. It always encourages and seeks the best for its object.

The Tragedies of Leadership Without God's Love

First Corinthians 13:1-3 reveals five areas in which God's love is essential or the results are ineffective in the lives of others. Roots as to why leaders fail to motivate others could be found in these verses.

A Speech Defect!

"If I speak with the tongues of men and of angels, but do not have love," says Paul, "I have become a noisy gong or a clanging cymbal" (v. 1). Leaders must talk. Hopefully, others will listen. If they don't, maybe the problem is the "speech defect" mentioned here: a lack of love. Linguistic ability and eloquence may be there, but God's love may be lacking.

I sat down in a plush office one day to talk with a leader about a particular area of disagreement. I was amazed at his eloquence, his command of the English language. But the longer he talked, the more uncomfortable I became. I had the feeling he really didn't care about my viewpoint or me personally. The feeling hurt, and I found myself failing to respond to what he was saying. I thought about how often that problem occurs when we talk with people. Sometimes that's all it is—just talk! No love. And it usually hurts.

Knowledge Alone Is "Arrogant"

First Corinthians 13:2 describes the problem of having great knowledge and understanding, but having no love. Leaders must know things. You can't lead out of ignorance. But it's important for knowledge to be accompanied by love—and it's a difficult balance!

First Corinthians 8:1 tells us, "Knowledge makes arrogant, but love edifies." It isn't better to be ignorant—that isn't the point! The point is that we need love with knowledge in order to be effective in the lives of others.

One staff member shared with me some time ago about one of her superiors that "he knows what he is talking about; he just doesn't care!" A common problem. Love is essential for knowledge to be helpful.

Faith Without Love Is Nothing

Leaders can't operate without faith! But, without love, they are nothing (see 1 Cor. 13:2). Removing mountains with faith is a tremendous gift! It's exciting to be around people with great faith.

Leaders with faith believe God can do things that most of us have never seen or experienced. Great mountains that seem like insurmountable obstacles to the Lord's work, come tumbling down before the faith of some leaders. Praise the Lord for faith like that! But, without love, the results are minimal in terms of affecting other people.

One pastor with whom I am acquainted challenged his people to great faith. He believed God could do what seemed to be impossible in a particular situation. The trouble is, he was way out in front of the people. He lost them in his zeal. He ran over them in his effort to see God do big

> *Some people are difficult to work with (in case you hadn't noticed). There are times when we must "put up" with them in love. After all, God puts up with us!*

things. The people were not with him, and the effort was a colossal failure.

What went wrong? The people felt he did not love them. They felt he just wanted to use them to build a great monument to his faith! Faith without love is a tragedy in leadership.

Loveless Giving Is Without Profit

Leaders should have giving hearts. They should share with people in time of need. But 1 Corinthians 13:3 reminds us that even if we give up our possessions "but do not have love, it profits me nothing." That's quite a statement! The need is certainly there. A sense of "charity" may be present. But without love, there is no profit. The act is not accomplishing what was intended. Charity without love does not do it. All the gifts in the world fail to minister to people when there is no love.

Martyrdom Without Love Is Wasted

Even if you gave your body to be burned—even if you became a martyr—it would be a waste of time, according to 1 Corinthians 13:3. Martyrdom for martyrdom's sake is not love. There are many occasions when we play the role of "martyr." This is no guarantee that we love people. It may be just a form of selfishness. People may become a martyr in a particular situation in order to receive attention, appreciation or recognition for what they have done. They want to be noticed.

All of these areas (speech, knowledge, faith, charity and martyrdom) are important; but without love they are not effective in the lives of others. Love enriches those things to the point of building up other people. Selfish motives turn to concern for others when love is controlling these areas. Tragedies in leadership can be changed to triumphs when God's love is operating.

WHAT DOES IT MEAN TO BE CONCERNED FOR OTHERS?

Leaders must show concern for others. You can't force it; it must come from the heart. But, how do you show concern like that? First Corinthians 13:4 reveals two qualities of God's love that reflect a concern for others rather than yourself.

Concern Implies Patience

What a simple statement "Love is patient"! When leaders are patient with others, people know we really are concerned for them. The Greek word for "patience" refers to taking a long time to boil. It's always used in reference to people, not things. God is never said to be patient toward things. He doesn't need that kind of patience. He is controlling all things! God does have patience toward people, however.

Ephesians 4:2 reminds us that patience toward people involves showing forbearance (literally, putting up with one another) toward one another in love. Some people are difficult to work with (in case you hadn't noticed) and to understand. There are times when we must "put up" with them in love. After all, God puts up with us—praise the Lord!

I was very impatient with one of our staff members. His speed and my speed were two different speeds! I wanted him to complete this task on my time schedule. I had a right to expect it from him—I was his boss! He did not finish it on time. He asked for more time. My impatience grew until I was sick of myself. Where was God's love? Absent! Instead of helping him, I was critical and impatient. Lord, forgive me!

The situation proved my lack of love. I asked God to forgive me, and tried another way. The other way demonstrated patience. The staff member thanked me for loving him. Will I ever learn?

The ability of leaders to motivate and challenge people will greatly deteriorate if the leader becomes impatient. God's love is patient toward people.

Being Concerned Is Being Kind

I like the sound of this word "kind." The Greek word in 1 Corinthians 13:4 is used of wine that is mellowed by age. Christ used the word when He said, "My yoke is easy" (Matt. 11:30). Submission to Him is not a heavy burden. The experienced ox carries the load. The inexperienced ox (believer) is trained to plow by being loosely tied to the yoke and simply learning from the experienced ox (Christ) alongside him.

Love is like that. It is easy on people, not harsh. It is willing to go alongside people and help them to learn and grow. Galatians 5:22 makes it a part of the "fruit of the Spirit." Ephesians 4:32 uses it with the idea of forgiving one another.

The root idea in the Greek word is that of usefulness. It's the opposite of harshness or bitterness. Leaders who understand kindness never seek to burden people down. They are easy to get along with and loving in their attitudes. They seek to help, not hurt.

Attitudes That Do Not Belong in a Leader's Life

If God's love is operating in the leader's life, there are certain attitudes that will not be evident. That's the point of 1 Corinthians 13:4-6, where eight negatives are listed. Here are eight things that love will not do.

Love Is Not Jealous

This word is often used in a good sense and translated "zeal." It is important to be zealous in areas that are good and productive. But zeal can lead to jealousy. The desire to have the same things for yourself that another person has is jealousy.

Leaders are guilty at times of comparing themselves with other leaders. They start wanting what someone else has. When it becomes a constant habit and begins to control you, you become intensely jealous. God's love is no longer working in your heart.

How do you handle the successes of others when they are brought to your attention? Learn to rejoice! God holds you responsible for what you have done and for what you can do, not for what someone else has done. Thank the Lord for His blessings on others and for the ministry they have. Don't start desiring it! After all, experience tells us that they've got problems you don't need or want!

Love Does Not Brag

Clement of Alexandria, an early church leader, said that bragging is ornamenting oneself with emphasis on the extraneous and useless! God's love has something to brag about, but not about that which is useless or self-centered.

God's love does not boast about achievements which God's grace has made possible, unless that boasting gives all the glory and credit to God Himself. It is quite easy to brag about things that do not really count in terms of human relationships or eternal values. God's love is different, and people notice!

The pastor who preceded me in my previous ministry (also my spiritual father) was showing me the new buildings that our church was constructing. I was considering the pastorate of the church at that time, but found myself a little hesitant about the awesome responsibilities and the possible debt that was being incurred by the congregation. Not knowing what to say, I said to him. "This is a tremendous undertaking. It must make you very proud to think this congregation could build such a large plant."

He responded by saying, "David, remember, the church is not the buildings. If the Lord comes tonight, the Antichrist is going to have a big debt!"

I don't remember whether that was encouraging to me at that time, but it sure put things in a proper perspective! I gave him the opportunity to brag a little, and he avoided it. Instead, I received an important lesson.

The buildings are not important. God's people are! Boasting in that which is extraneous or useless is a violation of God's love. It shows that our focus is wrong—it's on things, instead of people.

Love Is Not Arrogant

The Greek word for being arrogant means "to blow." It is used in the middle voice, meaning "to blow itself up." God's love does not parade in front of others, constantly inflating one's importance, abilities or achievements. Proverbs 27:2 says, "Let another praise you, and not your own mouth."

A sure sign of the lack of love is arrogance. Knowledge without love "puffs" or "blows itself up" (1 Cor. 8:1). Leaders can fall into this trap quite easily because they often have knowledge that others around them do not have.

Love Does Not Act Unbecomingly

To put it another way, God's love is not without shape. Our word "tact" would fit here. Etiquette is involved. God's love is not rude. It says the proper things at the proper time in the loving way.

Many of us mean well, but we are not concerned with how what we say affects others. We reveal that God's love is not controlling the way in which we say things to people. What you say may be good and right, but the manner in which you say it can greatly affect the way in which the people respond to you. Love is tactful.

Love Is Not Selfish

Seeking only our own good is not God's love. Wanting things your way is not love. God's love is filled with humility. It regards others as more important than yourself (see Phil. 2:3,4). What concerns others must be important to the spiritual leader.

The staff meeting we had one day was pursuing ideas for a particular ministry. Everyone was sharing what he or she felt was the best idea. It was good to a point. All of a sudden, we all felt a little selfish. We realized we were not concerned with how our ideas were affecting others.

It's amazing how quickly a time like that can change when another's viewpoint is considered! The ideas were then qualified and controlled. It became loving, rather than selfish. Wanting things our way comes naturally. We don't really have to work on it!

Love Is Not Provoked

The word "provoke" is based on the Greek word "to sharpen." Love is not made sharp by others. It does not get bitter by the reactions and criticisms of others.

Paul was provoked once. He was reacting to the idolatry of Athens (see Acts 17:16). But he was provoked at idolatry, not people. There is a world of difference! There are times when we ought to get upset and stirred about things and situations that are wrong and which clearly violate God's Word. But, God's love does not get upset with people. Spiritual leaders must learn the difference.

Love Overlooks Wrongs

When Paul wrote that "love does not take into account a wrong suffered," he was using the language of an accountant. The idea is that of calculating. God's love is forgiving, not holding a grudge against someone who has offended you. We are calculating when we let our minds dwell on the wrong that people have done to us. It's a form of self-centeredness. It is necessary to bury things that people do to us and to stop dwelling on them.

A friend shared with me one day that the reason he did what he did to a certain person was to get back at him for something that happened many years ago. How tragic! He carried a root of bitterness for many years. He calculated concerning the wrong done to him. He could not forgive, let alone forget.

Love Rejoices in Good, Not Evil
How do you react at the sight or sound of evil in others? God's love refrains from rejoicing, but rather is saddened. This phrase deals with a censorious spirit, one that condemns others for the sins in their lives.

It's easy to be glad at another's misfortune, especially when it might lead to your gain or will put you in a better

> *A spiritual leader protects and covers those who work with him. He sticks up for them, even though he knows there are problems in their lives.*

light before others. But this is not the way of God's love. God's love has no need of tearing others down in order to feel important. It doesn't rejoice at the failures of others.

One day our staff was discussing the problems of a church nearby. It was declining. We were taking comfort in the fact that our church was growing. It seemed that we were happy to hear of the other church's problems. I felt sick inside. It was wrong, and I knew it.

To help my own attitude, I put the other church's ministry on my prayer list and called the pastor one day to encourage him. My attitude changed. I really wanted him to succeed. The experience meant a great deal to me. In a small way, I felt love for him and his ministry. I've asked the Lord to help me to be sympathetic and compassionate when hearing of another's misfortune. Someday I may have a problem and I hope others will care.

How Do You React to Changing Circumstances?

God's love can help. Things don't always turn out the way we think or plan. When changes come, love can sustain us and encourage us. First Corinthians 13:7 mentions four things that will characterize our reactions to the "all things" of life when God's love is controlling.

Love Bears All Things

The Greek word means to protect or preserve by covering. In modern Greek it refers to the roof of a house. The idea here is that God's love puts up a shelter to shield or cover others.

There are many situations and circumstances in which this kind of reaction is needed in the life of the spiritual leader. He protects and covers those who work with him. He is their defender. He sticks up for them, even though he knows there are problems in their lives. His love is willing to bear these things when others would not be so patient. He concentrates on building people, and that takes time!

Love Believes All Things

This doesn't mean we're gullible or naive. It rather indicates a confidence and trust in everything that is happening. God is behind it all. It all has a purpose. This belief is the opposite of one who is always doubting things as to why they happen or should have happened.

A spiritual leader learns to rely upon God and His Word, not upon his feelings or whether things are going the way he planned. He trusts the sovereignty of God and knows that at times there will be "setbacks." These become stepping-stones when your trust is in the Lord.

The people who work for a spiritual leader who rests in the Lord, even in times of great stress and change, will find themselves coping with situations that might otherwise seem impossible to handle.

Love Hopes All Things

We must be optimistic. God's love looks to the future. It bases its response upon the character and power of God. God is able to do what to some seems impossible. Love always hopes for the best. It sees the "all things" as opportunities for God to work and demonstrate who He really is.

This kind of love is not easily discouraged. It's always trusting in what can be done, not dwelling on what was in the past or the trouble in the present. People respond readily to a love that hopes. They are encouraged. They will keep going in their work even under the most difficult circumstances.

Love Endures All Things

Love can take the pressure. The Greek word means "to remain under." It's used of things or situations, not people. Love bears up under difficult circumstances. It knows how to keep going when others drop out. It cares enough to stay when things are not going the way people want.

A pastor informed me that he was quitting his church. He was discouraged. The growth was not there that he wanted. He was impatient. He did not want to be associated with a declining church. I simply asked him, "Do you love these people?" He wasn't sure that was important. It was. God's love will keep you going when most people want to quit. God's love will endure under the most trying circumstances.

EXPERIENCING GOD'S LOVE

God's love is produced in our hearts through the presence and power of the Holy Spirit (see Rom. 5:5; Gal. 5:22). Every believer, because of the indwelling of the Holy Spirit (see 1 Cor. 6:19,20), has the capacity to experience God's love every day of his life. The potential is there. The application may be the problem. Being controlled by the Holy Spirit in order to love as God wants and as you need is the root problem in spiritual leadership. The great need is for Spirit-filled leaders.

Formulas have been suggested before as to how to experience a Spirit-filled life. Conditions such as prayer, faith, obedience, witness, study, etc., have all been proposed as "secrets" to a Spirit-filled life. It seems to fall in the category of what I call the "more syndrome." If I just do something "more" than what I'm doing now, I will achieve the desired result of being Spirit-filled. That can be very discouraging and self-defeating. How much is "more"? Do I need more prayer? Of course, always! Do I need more obedience? Of course, always!

To simplify this problem of being Spirit-filled, I began by recognizing that the Holy Spirit is God. He is fully capable of manifesting God's love in my life. He really doesn't need my help in one sense. I often get in the way of what He wants to do. I don't really need to worry about what He does.

Next, I realized that one thing stops the flow of God's power in my life—sin! It grieves and quenches the Spirit. My simple conclusion: Get rid of the sin and the filling of the Spirit is automatic! You may not like the simplicity of this, but it helps me, and it may help you. If sin stops the ministry of the Spirit, then that's the problem I need to deal with. Let's try an example for better understanding.

I had a problem showing love to a particular person. Everything I tried failed. Things got worse. One day I realized the problem: I had an unforgiving spirit toward something that person had done. Once that sin was removed, my love toward the person was restored. Very simple.

Another example: I deeply offended another staff member by an action I took as a spiritual leader. I felt at that time that I should apologize but I simply neglected to do so. Much later I discovered a serious problem in loving that staff member. Finally, after much internal struggle, I went to that person and apologized for what I had done many months before. The relationship was restored and love was now expressed freely between us.

The examples are numerous. Sin blocks the flow of God's love. Deal with sin, and you'll experience God's love again. Above all, don't put things off that you know you should do (like seeking forgiveness). Deal with things immediately. The love pattern will be more consistent.

☑ LEADER'S CHECKLIST

1. What attitudes do you have that do not belong in a leader's life?

2. Are you weak in any of the five areas in which God's love is essential? Which one(s)? What can you do to strengthen them?

3. How do you demonstrate patience and kindness?

4. Which of the eight negatives do you need to work on in your own life?

5. Is your love optimistic, looking to the future?

6. How do you react to changing circumstances?

7. How can you experience God's love in your life?

21

THE MARKS OF LOVING LEADERSHIP

IN the previous chapter we examined the love of God as described in 1 Corinthians 13 and applied it to leadership. In this chapter we will deal with other practical aspects of "loving leadership."

One of the greatest needs in the life of a spiritual leader is experiencing and expressing the love of God. Sixteen times in the New Testament we are told to "love one another." In the great passage of 1 John 4:7-19 on the love of God we are told the following:

1. God is love.
2. Love comes from God.
3. You must know God to have His love.
4. God's love was demonstrated when Jesus Christ died on the Cross for our sins.
5. Love is produced in us by the Holy Spirit of God.
6. Love is not afraid.
7. We are commanded to love one another.

8. Our capacity to love is based on the fact that God first loved us.

God's love is eternal and abiding—it lasts when other things fail (Jer. 31:3; 1 Cor. 13:8). It doesn't require a response in order to function (Rom. 5:8; 1 John 4:10) and it is never selfish or materialistic (1 John 2:15-16). God's love is compassionate toward the needs of others (1 John 3:17-18) and is concerned about the rights of others (Rom. 13:8-10). Its basic quality is that it is sacrificial (Eph. 5:2,25; 1 John 3:16; 4:9-10).

One of the most wonderful qualities about the love of God is that it is unconditional. It is based on God's faithfulness, not our worthiness or performance (Deut. 6:7-9; Lam. 3:22-24). It is also unconditional because of God's abundant mercy toward us (Ps. 103:8-11; Eph. 2:4) and His forgiveness (Prov. 10:12; 17:9; 1 Pet. 4:8). He simply and powerfully loves us! We can't earn or deserve such love...we merely accept it and respond to it.

It is wonderful to speak of the love of God, and to examine its marvelous traits and responses. Spiritual leaders need God's love in their lives and leadership. But it is helpful in understanding the marks of loving leadership to observe what it is that church leaders are responsible to do in the work of the Lord. Consider the following basic responsibilities.

SHEPHERDING THE FLOCK OF GOD

Perhaps no other statement so clearly reveals the role and responsibility of a church leader as this one important task. They are to be shepherds, lovingly caring for the flock entrusted to them.

In Acts 20:17-36 there is a moving passage about the

responsibility of the leaders in the church of Ephesus and their relationship to the apostle Paul. Paul instructed these leaders ("the elders of the church"—v. 17) to do the following: "Be on guard for yourselves and for all the flock, among which the Holy Spirit has made you overseers, to shepherd the church of God which He purchased with His own blood" (v. 28).

Guiding and Feeding

"To shepherd the church of God" is the responsibility of church leadership. A flock of sheep has a natural tendency to wander away (Isa. 53:6), and to get into lots of trouble and face much danger. The shepherd is lovingly to watch over them (as "overseers"), and to do all he can to protect and defend them (cf. Acts 20:28-30).

Peter, who describes himself as an elder, writes to fellow elders these words:

> Therefore, I exhort the elders among you, as your fellow elder and witness of the sufferings of Christ, and a partaker also of the glory that is to be revealed, shepherd the flock of God among you, exercising oversight not under compulsion, but voluntarily, according to the will of God; and not for sordid gain, but with eagerness; nor yet as lording it over those allotted to your charge, but proving to be examples to the flock. And when the Chief Shepherd appears, you will receive the unfading crown of glory (1 Pet. 5:1-4).

Loving leadership is concerned with feeding the flock of God. Such oversight is not forced, but willing and eager. The motive is not personal profit or the opportunity to be an authority over others. Church leaders are under-shepherds to Jesus Christ, who is the "Chief Shepherd" (1 Pet. 5:4; see also Ps. 23:1). It is His "well done" and His reward that we should desire.

Not "Lording It Over" the Flock

The negatives of this passage reveal the kind of leader where love is absent from what he says and does. This leader "lords" it over people. He lets them know who is in charge, and demands their submission. Hardly an example of loving leadership!

Several years ago one of the leaders in the church where I was pastoring was exercising his leadership with a strong hand. He spoke often of how people should submit to leadership, and he felt that I as a pastor should be preaching on submission to leadership more often in my sermons. He spoke of how rebellious people are. I noticed in several meetings that he dominated others and forced his opinions on the group.

It was obvious that people resented this man and the way he exercised his leadership. It came to him powerfully in one meeting when another brother who was being intimidated by him spoke out and confronted him: "You don't care about any other person but yourself! If you would show a little love once in a while, maybe more of us would listen to what you have to say!" The tension in that meeting was felt by every person in the room. No one knew what to say. The chairman dismissed us all with a word of prayer and an admonition to pray about this matter and to ask the Lord what He would have us to do.

At the next month's meeting, this domineering leader was a broken man. What he was told at the last meeting broke his heart, and for the first time in his life as a leader he saw himself as others did. He realized that his problem was a lack of love for people. He cared more about issues and things that had to be done, rather than for people. His public confession and request for forgiveness was warmly received by all the people in that meeting, and a wonderful time of prayer and encouragement followed. His leadership was different from that day onward.

MINISTRY TO THE NEEDY

Help with Material Needs

When church leaders were first selected in the church in Jerusalem, the problem which suggested the need for leadership was the care of widows. We read in Acts 6:1-3:

> Now at this time while the disciples were increasing in number, a complaint arose on the part of the Hellenistic Jews against the native Hebrews, because their widows were being overlooked in the daily serving of food. And the twelve summoned the congregation of the disciples and said, "It is not desirable for us to neglect the word of God in order to serve tables. But select from among you, brethren, seven men of good reputation, full of the Spirit and of wisdom, whom we may put in charge of this task."

Many denominations have concluded that these leaders are "deacons" and not "elders," because of the phrase "serve tables." However, there is no mention of deacons at this point nor in the early history of the church at Jerusalem.

In Acts 11:27-30, Christians in Antioch took up an offering to help those in Judea who were suffering from a famine. They sent it by the hands of Barnabas and Saul "to the elders," not deacons. Apparently, the elders were in charge of caring for those in need.

In 1 Timothy 5:1-6 there is a lengthy discussion about the care of widows and which ones of them should be supported by the church. Those without family support, and who had met certain qualifications of faithfulness to God and His church, were to be supported by the church. Verse 16 speaks about assisting those who are widows indeed.

> *Leaders who find fulfillment only in board meetings, reports and research, are failing to understand what God requires and His people need.*

The very next verses (1 Tim. 5:17ff.) deal with the responsibility of elders.

First John 3:17-18 speaks powerfully about caring for those in need:

> But whoever has the world's goods, and beholds his brother in need and closes his heart against him, how does the love of God abide in him? Little children, let us not love with word or with tongue, but in deed and truth.

Loving leadership will respond to human need. James 2:14-17 makes a similar point and relates it to saving faith:

> What use is it, my brethren, if a man says he has

faith, but he has no works? Can that faith save him? If a brother or sister is without clothing and in need of daily food, and one of you says to them, "Go in peace, be warmed and filled," and yet you do not give them what is necessary for their body, what use is that? Even so faith, if it has no works, is dead, being by itself.

Ministering to the Sick

The letter of James also indicates the responsibility of loving leadership toward those who suffer physically:

> Is anyone among you sick? Let him call for the elders of the church, and let them pray over him, anointing him with oil in the name of the Lord; and the prayer offered in faith will restore the one who is sick, and the Lord will raise him up, and if he has committed sins, they will be forgiven him. Therefore, confess your sins to one another, and pray for one another, so that you may be healed. The effective prayer of a righteous man can accomplish much. Elijah was a man with a nature like ours, and he prayed earnestly that it might not rain; and it did not rain on the earth for three years and six months. And he prayed again, and the sky poured rain, and the earth produced its fruit (Jas. 5:14-18).

Verse 14 indicates that the sick person is to call for the elders. The Greek word for "call" implies a private, not a public gathering. The sick person is to "call to himself" the elders of the church. They are to come to him, not the other way around.

The elders are instructed to anoint the sick person with oil and to pray for their healing. When Jesus sent out the Twelve on a preaching mission, we read that they "were anointing with oil many sick people and healing them" (Mark 6:13). Anointing with oil is not referring to the medicinal value of the oil. The oil symbolizes God's power and presence.

Notice that the text requires more than one elder. No one person is to be honored or praised for this ministry of healing. God is the one who heals. More than one elder insures that God gets the glory, not the elders. What saves or heals the sick person is the Lord. The text says, "the Lord will raise him up." The elders' part is prayer. It is not the sick person's lack of faith that results in a failure to heal. God is in sovereign control.

The elders are to pray with "the prayer offered in faith." It is not a prayer of demand. It is a word for worship, a quiet confidence in the living God who can do what He wants to do. It is not our great faith in God that heals; it is faith in a great God!

Leaders who manifest the love of God will help people in material and physical need. That is love. Anything less is not what God requires of spiritual leaders. Leaders who find fulfillment only in board meetings, reports and research, are failing to understand what God requires and His people need. It is much more than meetings, methods and materials; it is caring for people and doing what we can to meet their needs.

ADMONISHING AND CONFRONTING

Perhaps this responsibility is the most difficult. We do not often associate warning and confrontation with love. But that is the only way it can be done—with love.

Protecting the Flock

Paul speaks of a leader who is capable of "Holding fast the faithful word which is in accordance with the teaching, that he may be able both to exhort in sound doctrine and to refute those who contradict" (Titus 1:9). After pointing out the responsibility of church leaders Paul mentions the crucial nature of their confrontation in order to "silence" those who are "upsetting whole families" (v. 11).

In Acts 20:29-30, Paul advised the spiritual leaders in Ephesus:

> I know that after my departure savage wolves will come in among you, not sparing the flock; and from among your own selves men will arise, speaking perverse things, to draw away the disciples after them.

It is the responsibility of church leaders to protect the flock from attacks outside the ministry and from divisions within the ministry. Loving leadership cares about the flock and protects it, regardless of the personal criticism that they may receive because of it. No one wants to be confronted, but spiritual leaders must lovingly do so.

Paul again speaks of the confrontation issue when he states: "Brethren, even if a man is caught in any trespass, you who are spiritual, restore such a one in a spirit of gentleness; each one looking to yourself, lest you too be tempted" (Gal. 6:1). And in 1 Corinthians 4:14-16 he wrote these loving words about confrontation:

> I do not write these things to shame you, but to admonish you as my beloved children. For if you were to have countless tutors in Christ, yet you would not have many fathers; for in Christ Jesus I

became your father through the gospel. I exhort
you therefore, be imitators of me.

It is a loving father who confronts his children. He
warns and admonishes them, not because he is against
them and trying to limit their activities and enjoyment of
life; he does so to protect them from destroying their lives.

The Process of Church Discipline
The most difficult part of spiritual leadership is confronting
and warning believers of the consequences of their actions.
Church discipline is lacking all over the world. There is a
high degree of toleration for sinful behavior. The world's
relativism and secular thought has contributed to this mas-
sive problem. Individual rights are more important now
than corporate responsibility.

It is a difficult environment in which to confront people of wrongdoing. Most people do not want to hear about
it. They become extremely critical and insist that it is none
of our business. But, according to God's Word, it *is* our
business, and it must be done.

The process of confrontation and church discipline is
outlined clearly by our Lord:

> And if your brother sins, go and reprove him in
> private; if he listens to you, you have won your
> brother. But if he does not listen to you, take one or
> two more with you, so that by the mouth of two or
> three witnesses every fact may be confirmed. And
> if he refuses to listen to them, tell it to the church;
> and if he refuses to listen even to the church, let
> him be to you as a Gentile and a tax-gatherer. Truly
> I say to you, whatever you shall bind on earth shall
> be bound in heaven; and whatever you loose on

earth shall be loosed in heaven. Again I say to you, that if two of you agree on earth about anything that they may ask, it shall be done for them by My Father who is in heaven. For where two or three have gathered together in My name, there I am in their midst (Matt. 18:15-20).

Step 1: Personal and Private Confrontation. If there is a willingness to listen, acknowledge the sin and repent, then the goal is achieved. The love of the person confronting will cover the trespass (1 Pet. 4:8) and will not repeat it to anyone else.

It is at this point that many offenses occur. Often leaders will discuss a situation in a group or with one or two others before a private and personal confrontation has taken place. This leads to many rumors and false accusations. The more people involved at this point, the greater and more extensive is the harm done.

If the person does not listen to the private confrontation, then...

Step 2: Confrontation by Two or Three Witnesses. Sometimes a person will change his story or twist the facts or tell people that he did not say what the one person who confronted him said that he said. That's why two or three witnesses need to be involved when the sinning person does not respond to the personal and private confrontation of one person. Jesus' statement, "For where two or three have gathered together in My name, there I am in their midst" (Matt. 18:20), is referring to church discipline, not the basic gathering of a church!

If the person listens, then no further action needs to take place. It has been my experience that many people will confess what they have done, and truly "listen" to the confrontation at this point when there are two or more witnesses. Much of church discipline can be accomplished in the first two basic steps. If more ministries would carefully practice these steps in the order given, there would be less trouble in the public gatherings and less gossip and rumor developing over someone's sin.

Step 3: Tell It to the Church. It is hard to know what is meant here, especially since the church in Jerusalem came to number in the thousands. How could this be applied if it means all the members gathering for such a hearing? Perhaps in the smaller stages of growth when the church does not involve a great many people, this could be done.

It would seem likely that the leaders of the church would be the most appropriate group to deal with the situation. After the personal and private confrontation, and the situation involving two or three witnesses, the next step would involve the official governing body of the church, usually represented by the elders. This might explain the admonition of Titus 1:9 given to elders or bishops.

If the brother responds to this official confrontation and exposure, then praise the Lord! No more needs to be done, and the leaders should protect the individual from further damage and criticism.

Step 4: Let Him Be Excluded. At this point, the leadership has no other choice except to count the brother as an unbeliever—"as a Gentile and a tax-gatherer." That is, he is to be excluded from the fellowship and membership of the church. The purpose of such action is to restore the brother, not to get rid of a problem.

In 1 Corinthians 5 we have the incident of a church member at Corinth guilty of incest. The instruction was to remove the sinning brother from their fellowship. In verse 5, the apostle Paul admonishes them: "I have decided to deliver such a one to Satan for the destruction of his flesh, that his spirit may be saved in the day of the Lord Jesus."

Without the protective umbrella of the church, its members and its leadership, the sinning brother is now exposed to the consequences of his actions in a way not previously experienced. The interesting fact about this story is that the brother did repent. And in 2 Corinthians Paul urges the church to restore him and to demonstrate their love for him due to his repentance.

LEADING BY EXAMPLE

Hebrews 13:7 teaches: "Remember those who led you, who spoke the word of God to you; and considering the result of their conduct, imitate their faith." Peter wrote in 1 Peter 5:3 that the elders were to be "examples" to the flock. In 1 Timothy 5:17-18 Paul speaks of elders who rule:

> Let the elders who rule well be considered worthy of double honor, especially those who work hard at preaching and teaching. For the Scripture says, "You shall not muzzle the ox while he is threshing," and "The laborer is worthy of his wages."

In 1 Timothy 3:4-5, the qualifications for an elder's leadership ability arise out of his family life:

> He must be one who manages his own household well, keeping his children under control with all dignity (but if a man does not know how to manage his own household, how will he take care of the church of God?).

Here, managing the church is described by the words, "take care"—words used in Luke 10 in the story of the Good Samaritan who took care of the physical and material needs of a person beaten by robbers and left for dead. Loving leadership rules or leads by example and their family experience, managing the church with a heart to care for people and minister to their needs.

In all these matters, loving leadership takes place and demonstrates acts worthy of the title "spiritual leader." We need more leaders who know God's love and demonstrate it in all their responsibilities and actions toward people.

☑Leader's Checklist

1. List some of the qualities of God's love that you desire in your own life.
2. Why do you think many leaders lack love in their relationships with people?
3. Can you give a specific example of how a leader has shown love by what he has done? Was it received as a loving act?
4. What does it mean to "shepherd the flock"?
5. How can leaders help those in physical and material need?
6. Explain the steps of church discipline, and give illustrations if you can from your own experience.
7. How could your church strengthen its position and practice of church discipline?
8. Are you a spiritual leader? (Next chapter is crucial!)

22

THE BOTTOM LINE: ARE YOU A LEADER?

LEADERS are made, not born! That's the point behind this whole book. We named seven essentials that reveal what a spiritual leader is really like: example, communication, ability, motivation, authority, strategy and love. But how do you know for sure that you are a spiritual leader, especially if you've had no experience at leadership? Where do you start?

LEADERSHIP IS NOT FOR EVERYONE!

Some people believe that every person can be and should be a leader. If every person were a leader, who would do the following? No, leadership isn't for everyone. Experience shows that very clearly. Some people try to be leaders, only to discover that no one is following them. Others cannot take the pressure and demands of leadership. Some cannot make decisions or give direction to others. Some don't like the loneliness and isolation. Leadership really isn't for everyone!

There are degrees of leadership. Some do well with a group of 10 people but fail in leading 1,000 people. There are enormous differences in the leadership of 10 when compared with 1,000. The demands and responsibilities vary greatly.

There are different styles of leadership. Some like to work at desks, and some like motivating people to action. Some handle the training of the few, and others do well with motivating crowds. Some are rigid and inflexible; others are easy-going and constantly changing.

So, what is a leader, and how do you know if you are one? What is necessary to prove your leadership if you would like to be a leader but have no experience at it?

Leadership Evaluation

There are certain things by which leadership can be evaluated or tested. One of these tests by itself is not enough to prove you are a leader; but put together, they can help to confirm whether you are a leader or not.

Test 1—The Call of God

In spiritual leadership, it is imperative that a person knows that God has called him to a role of leadership. But how does God do that? Do you open the Bible and the first verse you see is the one that God will use to speak to you? Do you hear voices in the night? Does it come through a dream? Do you hear bells ringing? Does lightning flash from the sky? Of course not. Then how do you know if God has called you to spiritual leadership?

The call of God is a continual impression on your heart

that makes you desire to be a spiritual leader. If you really don't want to be a spiritual leader, then don't get involved. Concerning leaders for the local church, Paul wrote to Timothy that men should desire the office of leadership (see 1 Tim. 3:1).

The Greek text emphasizes an intense desire that a man feels in and of himself, not something that someone else

---

If God is calling you to be a leader, the desire should be strong and constant. If you can take it or leave it, then leave it.

---

has pressured him into doing. If God is calling you, the desire should be strong and constant. If it comes and goes, or if you can take it or leave it, then leave it. Don't get involved!

Test 2—Personal Desire
This flows out of the call of God. Do you want to be a leader? Do you really? Leaders who lack a strong personal desire for leadership are usually ineffective and weak leaders. You must really want it and enjoy it. Too many leaders complain about the responsibilities of leadership.

One of the men in our church was constantly complaining about his responsibilities as a leader. Everyone else was the problem, and his work load was too great to bear. He made it difficult for people to work with him. He was unbearable at times. He had a critical spirit. He did like the spiritual limelight that being a leader brought to him. He wanted to be noticed.

Today this man does not have a position of leadership. You might say he lost it. I would say it is doubtful that he ever had it. All the time he was in a position of leadership, he lacked the personal desire and joy of being a leader. One who has the desire enjoys the responsibilities of leadership and gladly assumes them.

Test 3—Maturity

Forget about spiritual leadership if you are still a baby Christian, or if you have not been growing in your knowledge of Christ. Maturity is essential for spiritual leadership. Maturity is necessary in order to discern whether or not you are a spiritual leader.

Just because you have had leadership in the secular world, do not conclude that spiritual leadership will come easy to you. Without maturity in Christ, you will fall flat on your face! You'll run into problems you never thought existed! You'll be hurt and often discouraged, and you'll probably give up in utter frustration!

Test 4—Experience

The old saying, "You'll never know until you try," would apply here. It's tough to know if you are a leader when you have never led anyone! Experience is vital to bringing you confidence and assurance of your spiritual leadership. Don't go through your Christian life wondering if you should or could have been a leader! Start experiencing it!

Start small. Don't go up to your pastor and say, "I would like to be the leader for that class of 200 people!" If he's smart, he won't give that kind of responsibility to someone without any experience as a spiritual leader. Take on a little responsibility within the framework of somebody else's leadership. Be faithful in a few things, and your leadership will grow to many things.

The most important thing to remember in gaining experience for spiritual leadership is to be faithful and dependable. It may be a small and insignificant ministry to you, but do it with all your heart! Those who are faithful in the small things have a way of being used in larger areas of ministry. Those who are not dependable, in spite of having many opportunities, never become strong spiritual leaders.

Test 5—Confirmation by Others

Does anyone else think you are a leader (besides your father and mother!)? Before you judge whether you are a spiritual leader or not, you'd better consider what others are saying. That's why time is necessary in evaluating spiritual leaders. It takes time to observe people in action. It takes time to determine faithfulness and dependability.

A few years ago, one of the young men in our church felt that God wanted him to be a spiritual leader. He communicated that to us, as he should have done. But one thing was missing: confirmation by others. When people were asked concerning his effectiveness, much doubt and question about him were expressed. We waited a little longer (good advice!).

The people in the area of ministry where he was working were not convinced of his leadership. Maybe they were wrong. Perhaps it was something personal. Let's give him the benefit of a doubt. We checked with others in another area of ministry. Same report. Much doubt as to whether he was a leader was continually reflected in these discussions. Our only choice? We decided not to use him in a particular leadership role until his spiritual leadership became more evident to those with whom he worked.

The counsel of other members of the Body of Christ is vital to the determination of spiritual leadership. If everyone questions the person's leadership, it is doubtful that any effective leadership can be exercised!

Test 6—Results
Are there any results occurring from the exercise of your leadership? Were goals reached? Were people challenged, discipled and enlisted? Was the response of the people positive?

Goals that are specific and measurable are vital to determining the results of spiritual leadership. Goals form a solid basis for evaluation.

One summer I saw a man's leadership exercised in a most revealing way as he mobilized, on his own, over 500 people to do some maintenance work on our church facilities. Some may have questioned his leadership but the results proved he was a leader! He accomplished the goals he set out to complete within the time period designated and the funds allowed.

Results can be seen in the lives of people whom the spiritual leader has trained and motivated. Are they productive people? That speaks well for the leadership of the one who poured his time and energy into them. It isn't always noticed by outsiders, but real leadership can be evaluated by how effective the people are who work for him or under him.

Other results to be evaluated are efficiency and happiness among those working with the leader. When things are in constant turmoil, there is a question about the leadership.

Test 7—Knowledge
What do you know about leadership? Have you read books on it? They will help. None of them are the final answer to being a leader, but they won't hurt you! Have you attend-

ed any leadership seminars or conferences? What principles of leadership and management do you know?

It is my personal conviction that seminaries and graduate schools preparing people for spiritual leadership should have courses in their curriculum that deal with spiritual leadership. These courses should not only require reading in the fields of leadership and management, but should also seek ways to give students valuable experience in exercising leadership.

Learn all you can about leadership. There are many books available (both sacred and secular). Learn also from the lives of those who are spiritual leaders. Study what they do and how they do it. Learn from the many biblical examples of spiritual leaders. Knowledge of leadership will aid you in the development of your own leadership.

CHECKING THE EVIDENCE

Take these seven tests, then evaluate yourself on the chart below. Is the evidence of each test strong, meaning a continual thing with you? Or is it weak, meaning that the test can only be applied in a few situations? The category of "weak" would indicate the necessity of more time and opportunity for evaluation. Maybe the evidence is not there yet in your life. If so, mark the category "none."

Tests of Leadership	Evidence		
	None	Weak	Strong
1. The call of God	☐	☐	☐
2. Personal desire	☐	☐	☐
3. Maturity	☐	☐	☐
4. Experience	☐	☐	☐
5. Confirmation by others	☐	☐	☐
6. Results	☐	☐	☐
7. Knowledge	☐	☐	☐

Don't be discouraged by past experience or present difficulties. The Lord can make you the leader He wants you to be! Trust Him, and rely upon His power and strength! If leadership is your desire, pray every day that God would develop and strengthen your leadership. Ask Him to give you wisdom for that leadership.

Sometimes you will feel that being a leader is not worth it. You will receive complaints and criticisms from people because you are in the position of leadership. Everything won't turn out the way you expected or planned. There will be conflicts and personality problems. People will get upset and hurt over the way you handle things. Others will oppose you and resist your leadership. It will be easy at times to say "I quit." Remove those words from your vocabulary right now! Never quit! You may change things or situations, but don't ever quit!

One day it will be worth it all to hear our Savior say, "Well done, good and faithful servant." It is His approval that we want! It's worth it, my leader friend, not only for future reward but for present blessing.

Leadership is not easy, but it's worth it! I love it. Do you? I wouldn't want things different in my life in terms of leadership. I want to be a leader. I don't deserve to be, but I want it! I want to do the best job I possibly can for the glory of my Lord Jesus Christ! I need His help every day, and that's obvious to all who work with me! I'm not perfect, and I don't know all there is to know about leadership. But, I'm trying. I'm working at it, and so should you! We all can learn. Every person and every situation is our teacher!

Leaders are made, not born! Therefore, there's hope for all of us! The Lord can make us into the leaders He wants us to be! Praise His wonderful name! ❧